The Joy of Less

A COMPASSIONATE GUIDE TO DECLUTTERING AND ORGANIZING, AND SUPPORTING OTHERS THROUGH LIFE TRANSITIONS

SOPHIE ALDEN

Copyright © 2025 by Sophie Alden

All rights reserved.

No portion of this book may be reproduced in any form without written permission from the publisher or author, except as permitted by copyright law.

This publication is designed to provide accurate and authoritative information in regard to the subject matter covered. It is sold with the understanding that neither the author nor the publisher is engaged in rendering legal, investment, accounting or other professional services. While the publisher and author have used their best efforts in preparing this book, they make no representations or warranties with respect to the accuracy or completeness of the contents of this book and specifically disclaim any implied warranties of merchantability or fitness for a particular purpose. No warranty may be created or extended by sales representatives or written sales materials. The advice and strategies contained herein may not be suitable for your situation. You should consult with a professional when appropriate. Neither the publisher nor the author shall be liable for any loss of profit or any other commercial damages, including but not limited to special, incidental, consequential, personal, or other damages.

First edition 2025

Contents

Introduction	1
1. Creating Your Personal Decluttering Blueprint Strategies for Success	3
2. Navigating Emotional Attachments A Compassionate Approach to Letting Go	27
3. The Sentimental Items Solution Creative Ways to Preserve Memories	51
4. Family Dynamics and Downsizing Managing Relationships Through Change	73
5. The Life Simplification Method Organizing What Remains	99
6. Sustaining Your Clutter-Free Transformation Building Lasting Habits	123
Conclusion	145

References	149
Also by Sophie Alden	151
Featuring Sophie Alden's Premiere DIY Book ~~Available through Amazon, Chapters Indigo, Barnes and~~ Noble, Kobo, and Ingram Spark	153
About the author Sophie Alden	155

Introduction

IN THE QUIET EARLY hours, when the world is just beginning to stir and sunlight filters through the kitchen window, I find myself reflecting on the path that led me here—to this book, and to this conversation with you.

Like many people, my journey toward a simpler life began with a feeling of overwhelm. Not just from too many belongings, but from the quiet weight that clutter carries—decisions to make, memories to process, and responsibilities attached to every object we hold onto.

Over time, through my own experience of downsizing—and through helping friends and older relatives do the same—I began to realize that living with less isn't just about letting go of things. It's about changing the way we see our belongings, and how we decide what truly has a place in our lives. Whether I was sitting with a friend as we sorted through a lifetime of keepsakes or supporting a neighbor preparing for a move, each experience deepened my understanding of how personal and emotional this process can be.

I often think about my mother, standing in her living room surrounded by three generations of our family's belongings. She picked up her grandmother's teacup and held it carefully, eyes filling with tears. That moment stayed with me—not because of the object itself, but because of the emotions it carried. The process of simplifying our homes is rarely just about organizing. It's about making space for memories, meaning, and the life we're living now.

This book isn't just a guide to clearing out clutter. It's a thoughtful, supportive resource for anyone who's ready to create more space—physically, mentally, and emotionally. Whether you're downsizing by choice or circumstance, going through a transition, or simply hoping to bring more peace into your day-to-day life, these pages offer practical tools, gentle encouragement, and a sense of direction.

Together, we'll walk through both the practical and emotional sides of this process—how to sort and organize, how to preserve what matters most, and how to navigate the sometimes tender moments that come with letting go. You'll find guidance, tools, and real-life stories along the way.

This isn't about getting everything perfect. It's about creating a home—and a life—that feels lighter, calmer, and more aligned with what matters most to you.

Let's begin, one thoughtful step at a time.

Chapter One

Creating Your Personal Decluttering Blueprint

Strategies for Success

Creating a decluttering blueprint isn't about sticking to a rigid, one-size-fits-all plan. It's about shaping a personalized strategy that fits your life—your routines, your energy levels, and your unique goals. Just like an architect sketches every detail of a structure with care and purpose, we'll build your own decluttering plan with that same thoughtful intention.

This isn't about forcing yourself into a system that doesn't feel natural. It's about working with your life, not against it. If you come up with a plan that reflects the way you actually live—rather than some idealized version of it—you're far more likely to stick with it. Your blueprint should feel like a flexible guide, not a strict set of rules. Life changes, energy fluctuates, and unexpected things pop up. A strong blueprint gives you structure, but also the breathing room to adjust along the way.

I saw this in action while working with my cousin and her family. Nancy is a hospital physiotherapist juggling long shifts and a busy household. Their kids has grown and their home was still full of stuff they didn't need which left little space for the things she did want space for. She had tried a few popular organizing methods before but found herself frustrated. They didn't match the rhythm of her daily life so they weren't successful. The room-by-room approach, for example, just didn't work for a family constantly moving between school drop-offs, work schedules, and evening commitments.

So, we tried something different. Together, we created what we called the "15-minute zones" system—breaking the house into smaller, manageable sections that could be tackled in short bursts of time. Instead of dedicating hours to one space, We focused on quick wins in targeted areas.

It worked beautifully. Three months later, not only had they cleared lots of space in their home, they were keeping it that way—because the system made sense for their lifestyle. That experience was a powerful reminder: the most successful decluttering strategies aren't necessarily the most popular ones—they're the ones that meet you where you are.

In this chapter, we'll explore how to create your own customized decluttering strategy that aligns with your lifestyle, goals, and emotional readiness. You'll discover practical methods for evaluating your space, setting realistic timelines, and developing sustainable systems that complement your daily life. Whether you're a busy professional, a parent managing multiple schedules, or someone preparing for a significant life transition, the principles and tools we'll cover can be adapted to fit your unique situation.

Remember, the goal isn't to achieve some idealized version of perfection – it's to make consistent, meaningful progress toward the simplified life you envision. Your decluttering journey is uniquely yours, and it doesn't need to follow anyone else's timeline or standards. By the end of this chapter, you'll have the framework and confidence to begin crafting your personal decluttering blueprint, one that will not only guide you through the initial clearing process but also help you maintain your simplified space for years to come.

Assessing Your Current Space and Lifestyle Needs

Before diving into the decluttering process, it's important to take a thoughtful inventory of your current living situation and daily routines. This assessment isn't just about measuring square footage or counting rooms – it's about understanding how you actually use your space and what you truly need to thrive. From my own downsizing journey and experiences helping others, I've learned that trying to force ourselves into organizational systems that don't align with our natural habits rarely leads to lasting change.

Let me share a personal example that transformed how I think about space assessment. Several years ago, while evaluating my home office, I discovered that I had been fighting against my natural work patterns. I had a beautiful desk positioned exactly where conventional wisdom suggested – by a window with plenty of natural light. However, I consistently found myself working at my kitchen table instead. Rather than trying to force myself to use the 'proper' workspace, I recognized this pattern and redesigned my office to mirror the elements that drew me to the kitchen – ample surface area, easy access to her reference materials and less direct light that made it easier to see my computer screen.

To begin your own space assessment, I recommend what I call the 'Living Space Journal' exercise. For one week, carry a small notebook and document moments of friction in your space – times when you can't find something, when you feel cramped, or when your environment isn't supporting your needs. Pay special attention to:

- Your daily traffic patterns through your home

- Spots where clutter consistently accumulates

- How effectively your current storage solutions serve you

- Whether your space supports your daily activities and routines

- Any upcoming life changes that might affect your space needs

When I conducted this exercise in my own home, it revealed some surprising things about how I actually used my space versus how I thought I used it. I discovered I was holding onto a formal dining set that hadn't been used in over a year, while lacking adequate space for my daily yoga practice. This realization helped me make the decision to let go of the dining set and create a dedicated wellness area that better served my lifestyle.

Consider also the seasonal rhythms of your life. How does your space need to function differently during various times of the year? For instance, I noticed my entryway is used quite differently in summer (when it's filled with gardening supplies) and winter (when it needs to accommodate boots and cold-weather gear). Understanding this pattern helped me create a more adaptable and functional living environment.

The key is to observe your space with curiosity rather than judgment. Think of yourself as a researcher studying your own habitat. Notice which areas of your home feel energizing and which feel draining. Where do you naturally gravitate when you need to relax? Where do you find yourself avoiding? These observations provide valuable clues about how to create an environment that truly supports your life.

As you conduct your assessment, remember that this isn't about finding fault with your current setup – it's about gathering information to make informed decisions about your space. Pay particular attention to:

- The times of day when different spaces are most used

- Storage areas that are difficult to access or maintain

- Rooms or areas that aren't serving their intended purpose

- Spaces that make you feel calm and productive

- Areas that consistently cause stress or frustration

Through helping elderly couples downsize their homes and working with friends and family members on their decluttering journeys, I've observed that those who take time for this thorough assessment phase make more sustainable decisions throughout their downsizing process. They're less likely to regret letting go of items and more successful in maintaining their organized spaces because their solutions are tailored to their actual needs rather than an idealized version of how they think they should live.

Your space assessment will serve as the foundation for all your future downsizing decisions. By understanding how you truly live in your space, you can create an environment that actively supports the life you want to lead, rather than one that simply looks organized on the surface.

Creating a Room-by-Room Priority System

Creating a systematic approach to downsizing begins with establishing a clear priority system for tackling different areas of your home. Through my family's own downsizing journey and helping friends navigate their transitions, I've discovered that randomly bouncing between rooms often leads to overwhelm and scattered results. A structured room-by-room approach helps maintain focus and build momentum throughout your downsizing journey.

When my elderly neighbor asked for help downsizing her home, we initially started with her attic full of family heirlooms and memories. This emotionally charged beginning quickly led to decision fatigue and temporarily halted our progress. From this experience, I learned that starting with less emotionally loaded spaces allows you to build your decision-making muscles before tackling more challenging areas.

Here are the key factors to consider when prioritizing rooms:

- **Frequency of Use:** Start with spaces you use daily

- **Emotional Investment:** Begin with less emotionally charged areas

- **Quick Win Potential:** Identify rooms where visible progress can be made quickly

- **Seasonal Timing:** Consider weather and seasonal factors that might affect the process

- **Current Functionality:** Prioritize spaces that aren't serving their intended purpose

I saw the power of this approach when helping my friend Lisa downsize her home. Instead of diving straight into her late mother's craft room – which she'd been avoiding for months – we began with her guest bathroom. This space had minimal emotional attachment but was cluttered with expired products and duplicate items. The confidence she gained from this smaller project provided the momentum she needed to gradually work through more challenging spaces.

A practical way to implement your room-by-room priority system is through what I call the 'Zone Impact Assessment.' Draw a simple floor plan of your home and rate each area on a scale of 1-3 for both emotional attachment and daily impact. Areas with high daily impact but low emotional attachment make excellent starting points. This creates a clear roadmap for your downsizing journey while acknowledging the emotional aspects of the process.

Consider breaking larger rooms into smaller, manageable zones. For instance, rather than tackling your entire kitchen at once, break it down into specific areas like:

- Upper cabinets
- Lower cabinets
- Pantry
- Countertop surfaces
- Appliance storage

This approach prevents overwhelm and allows you to maintain functionality in frequently used spaces while working through your priority system. During my own kitchen downsizing, breaking the space into zones helped me maintain our family's daily routines while still making steady progress.

Your priority system should remain flexible enough to accommodate life's unexpected changes. When helping my sister's family downsize, we had to adjust our room sequence when her elderly father-in-law needed to move in unexpectedly. The ability to adapt your priority system while maintaining overall progress is crucial for long-term success.

As you develop your room-by-room priority system, maintain a balance between progress and practicality. It might be tempting to tackle your biggest challenge first, but building confidence through smaller successes often leads to more sustainable results. Think of it as training for a marathon – you don't start with the full distance; you build up your endurance gradually.

Document your progress as you move through each space. This not only provides motivation but also helps identify patterns in your decision-making process that can be applied to future rooms. Take before and after photos, not just for satisfaction, but as a practical reference for maintaining the systems you create in each space. Through my own downsizing efforts, I've found that these visual records serve as powerful reminders of how far you've come and help maintain momentum when facing challenging spaces.

Developing Your Personal Decision-Making Framework

One of the most crucial elements of successful downsizing is developing a clear and consistent framework for making decisions about your possessions. When I first began my own downsizing journey, I found myself stuck in endless loops of 'maybe I'll need this someday' thinking. It wasn't until I developed a specific set of questions to guide my decisions that I began making real progress.

This framework became what I now call the 'Purpose and Joy Filter' - a system that evaluates items based on both their practical utility and their ability to contribute to our well-being.

Through helping three elderly couples downsize their homes and assisting countless friends with their decluttering journeys, I've witnessed how having a structured approach can transform the downsizing process from overwhelming to manageable.

Here are the foundational questions I've found most effective in an decision-making framework:

- Does this item serve a clear purpose in my current life?

- Have I used this item in the past year?

- Does keeping this item align with my vision for my simplified life?

- Would I buy this item again today?

- Does this item bring genuine joy or value to my daily life?

Let me share a story about my friend Emma, who transformed her decision-making process during her downsizing journey. Initially, she struggled with every item, spending precious time deliberating over even the smallest things. Together, we created what she called her 'Three-Breath Rule' - if she couldn't decide about an item within three deep breaths, it went into a temporary holding box. This simple framework freed her from decision paralysis and helped her maintain momentum throughout her downsizing project.

Your decision-making framework should reflect your personal values and lifestyle goals. For instance, if sustainability is important to you, you might add questions about an item's environmental impact or potential for reuse. If you're downsizing to travel more, your framework might emphasize portability and essential functions.

I recommend starting with a practice session in a low-stakes area, like your sock drawer or bathroom cabinet. Use this space to refine your decision-making criteria and build confidence in your judgment. Pay attention to how different questions resonate with you and adjust your framework accordingly.

One particularly effective technique I've developed is the 'Future Self Conversation.' When making decisions about items, imagine having a conversation with yourself five years from now. Would your future self thank you for keeping this item, or would they wish you had created more space for new experiences and possibilities?

Here are some practical guidelines for implementing your framework:

- Set specific timeframes for decision-making
- Create clear categories for items (keep, donate, sell, discard)
- Establish a designated space for uncertain items
- Document decisions to help identify patterns
- Review and adjust your framework regularly

Remember that your decision-making framework isn't just about getting rid of things - it's about creating a thoughtful process for curating your possessions. This framework will serve you not only during your initial downsizing but also in maintaining your simplified lifestyle moving forward.

During my own downsizing journey, I discovered that having a *consistent decision-making framework* led to more confident choices and less regret about items I chose to let go. The same has been true for friends and family members I've helped through their downsizing processes - those who develop and stick to a consistent decision-making framework complete their projects more successfully and maintain their organized spaces more effectively.

Your framework should also include a component for handling exceptions - those items that don't fit neatly into your usual criteria. Perhaps it's family heirlooms or specialized equipment for hobbies. Create clear guidelines for these categories while maintaining the spirit of your overall simplification goals.

As you develop your framework, be patient with yourself. Decision-making muscles strengthen with practice, and what feels challenging at first will become more natural over time. The goal isn't to make perfect decisions but to make consistent, intentional choices that align with your vision for a simplified life.

Establishing Realistic Timelines and Milestones

One of the most important things I've learned through my own efforts to downsize and declutter, as well as helping others streamline their lives, is that realistic timelines are essential for success. When I helped my neighbors downsize their home of forty years, I witnessed firsthand how hasty timelines can derail even the most motivated efforts. They initially wanted to complete everything in two weekends! This rushed approach left them overwhelmed and discouraged. Together, we developed a more balanced timeline that respected both their physical energy levels and emotional needs.

Here are some factors to consider when establishing your timeline:

- Your current schedule and daily commitments

- Physical and emotional energy levels

- Size and complexity of your space

- Emotional attachment to items

- Available help and support

- Seasonal factors and weather considerations

I use what I call the 'Progressive Timeline Approach,' which breaks down your downsizing project into three main phases: planning, active downsizing, and refinement. Each phase should have clear milestones that are both achievable and measurable. For example, during the planning phase, completing your space assessment and creating your decision-making framework are concrete milestones that set you up for success.

When my friend Sarah approached me about downsizing her home office, we developed what we called the '2-2-2 Method'

- spending two hours, two days a week, for two months. This structured approach helped prevent burnout while maintaining steady progress. The key was building in reflection points. These are scheduled pauses to assess progress and adjust the plan as needed.

Consider breaking your timeline into these manageable segments:

- Initial Assessment and Planning (1-2 weeks)

- High-Traffic Areas (2-3 weeks)

- Storage Spaces (2-3 weeks)

- Sentimental Items (3-4 weeks)

- Final Organization and Systems Implementation (2 weeks)

Remember that these timeframes are guidelines, not rigid rules. Your personal timeline might need to be longer or shorter depending on your specific circumstances. What's most important is being realistic about what you can accomplish while maintaining your daily responsibilities and emotional well-being.

Last spring, I helped my friend Sylvie, a busy mother of two, create a downsizing timeline that worked around her children's school schedule. Instead of attempting marathon decluttering sessions on weekends, we broke her project into 30-minute morning sessions and occasional longer blocks when she had childcare. This personalized approach allowed her to make steady progress without feeling overwhelmed.

When establishing milestones, make them specific and measurable. Instead of a vague goal like 'clean out the garage,' break it down into concrete tasks such as 'sort and categorize tools' or 'clear workbench area.' This specificity makes the process less daunting and provides clear markers of progress.

It's very important to build flexibility into your timeline. Life has a way of throwing unexpected challenges our way, and a rigid timeline can lead to frustration and abandonment of the project. I always recommend adding a 20% buffer to estimated timeframes to account for unexpected events or emotional processing needs.

Your timeline should also include specific dates for decision-making about items in your 'maybe' pile. Without these deadlines, uncertain items can linger indefinitely, preventing you from fully completing your downsizing project. Set reasonable time limits for revisiting these items, knowing that you can always adjust these dates if needed.

Finally, celebrate your progress along the way. Each completed milestone, no matter how small, represents a step toward your simplified living goals. These celebrations help maintain momentum and provide encouragement during challenging phases of your downsizing journey. Whether it's taking before-and-after photos or sharing your progress with supportive friends, acknowledging your achievements helps sustain motivation for the long term.

Building Sustainable Organization Systems

Creating sustainable organization systems is about developing intuitive solutions that work with your natural tendencies rather than against them. Through my own experience I've discovered that the most effective systems are those that feel almost effortless, supporting daily routines while preventing the gradual accumulation of clutter.

When I helped my friend Emma organize her home after a major downsize, we focused on what I call the 'Natural Flow Method' - observing how she naturally moved through her space and placing items accordingly. Rather than forcing herself to adopt complex organizational systems, we created simple solutions that aligned with her existing habits. For instance, we noticed she always dropped her keys and mail on the kitchen counter, so we installed a small, attractive command center in that exact spot rather than trying to change her routine.

The key elements of building sustainable organization systems include:

- Designated zones for specific activities and items

- Clear, visible storage solutions

- Simple maintenance routines

- Flexible systems that can adapt to changing needs

- Built-in space for future items

Through helping elderly couples downsize and assisting friends with their organizational challenges, I've learned that the most sustainable systems follow what I call the 'Maximum Accessibility Principle'

- keeping frequently used items easily visible and accessible while storing less-used items in less convenient locations.

Let me share a practical example from my own home. In my kitchen, I noticed I was constantly shuffling through stacked pans to reach the ones I used most often. Instead of maintaining this frustrating system, I installed a simple wall-mounted rack that displays my essential cookware within easy reach. This small change not only saved time but also prevented the disorganization that occurred when items were difficult to access.

One of the most effective techniques I've used is a 'Zone Mapping Exercise.' Start by observing your daily patterns for a week, noting where you naturally place items and how you move through your space. Then, design your organizational systems around these patterns, making small optimizations rather than wholesale changes. This approach leads to significantly higher success rates in maintaining organization long-term.

Consider these foundational principles when building your sustainable organization systems:

- **Visibility**: Keep frequently used items easily accessible
- **Simplicity:** The fewer steps required, the more likely you'll maintain the system
- **Flexibility:** Allow for adjustments as your needs change
- **Intuitive Flow**: Organization should feel natural, not forced

- **Regular Review:** Schedule periodic system evaluations

Remember that sustainable organization isn't about achieving perfection - it's about creating systems that support your lifestyle while requiring minimal effort to maintain. Think of it as setting up your future self for success. Every organizational decision should pass what I call the 'Tomorrow Test': Will this be easy to maintain tomorrow, next week, and next month?

Your organization system should also include clear protocols for bringing new items into your space. I recommend using the 'One In, One Out' method - for every new item that enters your space, remove one similar item. This prevents gradual accumulation while maintaining the functionality of your systems.

Build in regular maintenance checkpoints - weekly resets, monthly reviews, and seasonal adjustments. These rhythmic check-ins help catch small issues before they become overwhelming problems. They also provide opportunities to refine your systems based on changing needs and circumstances.

Remember, the goal isn't to create a showcase-worthy space that's impossible to maintain. Instead, focus on developing systems that support your daily life while gently encouraging better organizational habits. When done correctly, these systems should feel like helpful friends rather than demanding taskmasters.

Implementing the 'One In, One Out' Rule for Long-term Success

The 'One In, One Out' rule represents one of the most powerful yet simple principles for maintaining a clutter-free life after downsizing. This straightforward concept – when you bring something new into your space, something else must go – creates a natural boundary that prevents the gradual accumulation of possessions while preserving the freedom you've worked so hard to achieve.

I discovered the transformative power of this rule during my own downsizing journey, particularly in managing my book collection. As an avid reader, I found my shelves continuously expanding until I implemented this principle. Now, when I bring home a new book, I thoughtfully choose one to pass along to someone else who might enjoy it. This practice has transformed my relationship with acquisitions, making each new addition a mindful decision rather than an automatic yes.

Success with the 'One In, One Out' rule depends on establishing clear guidelines from the start. Here are the essential elements that make this rule sustainable:

- **Create a Pre-Purchase Pause**: Before acquiring something new, identify what item it will replace

- **Maintain a Running Inventory**: Keep track of key categories where accumulation tends to occur

- **Establish Category Limits**: Set maximum numbers for specific types of items

- **Schedule Regular Assessments:** Review your belongings quarterly to ensure balance

- **Document Your Exchanges**: Keep a simple log of items entering and leaving your space

The key to making this rule sustainable is understanding that it's not about deprivation – it's about mindful curation of your possessions. Think of your home as having a fixed number of 'spots' for items, similar to a carefully curated museum collection. When a new piece arrives, it should truly earn its place by being more valuable or useful than what it's replacing.

I've found particular success with what I call the 'Seasonal Swap' approach. Rather than making immediate decisions about removing items when something new comes in, keep a dedicated space for recent acquisitions. At the end of each season, review these items alongside their potential replacements, making more informed decisions about what truly deserves to stay in your life.

The 'One In, One Out' rule becomes especially powerful when applied to specific categories where we tend to over-accumulate. For example, in my home, we maintain category limits for kitchen tools and decorative items. This focused approach helps prevent the subtle creep of clutter in areas where it's most likely to occur.

Remember that this rule should be applied with flexibility and compassion. There will be exceptions and special circumstances, and that's okay. The goal isn't perfect adherence but rather creating a sustainable framework for maintaining your simplified space. I often remind friends that it's better to consistently follow this rule 80% of the time than to attempt perfect compliance and give up entirely.

To help maintain this practice, I recommend creating 'Decision Zones' in your home – designated areas where new items wait before being fully incorporated into your space. This pause gives you time to thoughtfully consider what might need to leave to make room for the new addition. It also helps prevent impulse purchases from undermining your organizational systems.

The success of the 'One In, One Out' rule often depends on how well it's integrated into your daily routines. Consider establishing regular check-in points, such as weekly reviews of new acquisitions or monthly assessments of specific categories. These rhythmic evaluations help ensure the rule becomes a natural part of your lifestyle rather than a burdensome chore.

Through my own experience and helping others, I've found that maintaining this rule becomes easier when you don't view it as a restriction. Instead, view it as a tool for preserving the spaciousness and order you've created. It's about making conscious choices that support your vision of a simplified, intentional life. Each time you successfully implement this rule, you're reinforcing your commitment to living with less and choosing quality over quantity.

Remember that the ultimate goal of the 'One In, One Out' rule isn't to restrict your life but to enhance it by maintaining the spaciousness and order you've worked so hard to achieve. When implemented thoughtfully, it becomes less about rigid rules and more about conscious choices that support your vision of a simplified, intentional life.

As we conclude this chapter on creating your personal declutter freedom blueprint, let me share what I've learned from helping friends, family and neighbors through their downsizing journeys - *the most effective strategies are the ones that work with your natural tendencies and respect your unique circumstances.* Throughout this chapter, we've explored how to develop personalized systems, from assessing your space to building sustainable organization methods. We've seen how breaking projects into manageable chunks, like my cousin Nancy's '15-minute zones,' can transform overwhelming tasks into achievable goals.

The journey of creating your decluttering blueprint begins with a bit of honest self-reflection and grows through thoughtful, practical planning. I've seen how personalized strategies are the ones that truly last. Whether you're experimenting with the Zone Mapping Exercise or adapting the Natural Flow Method to fit your rhythm, remember: your blueprint should reflect your life, not someone else's version of what simplicity should look like.

This isn't just a checklist or a one-time project. Your blueprint is a living document—something that can grow and shift as your needs evolve and your confidence builds. When you start applying simple, sustainable systems—like the One In, One Out guideline—it's less about sticking to strict rules and more about developing a thoughtful, intentional approach to the things you welcome into your space.

What matters most isn't how fast you can clear a room—it's how well your systems support the kind of life you want to live. Whether you choose the 2-2-2 Method or create a timeline of your own, steady, intentional progress will always carry you farther than quick fixes.

As you begin putting your plan into action, trust yourself. Your blueprint is more than a guide to organizing your home—it's a tool for shaping a life with more clarity, ease, and intention. Every step you take, no matter how small, is a meaningful part of that process.

In the next chapter, we'll step into the emotional side of this journey—how to gently navigate our attachments to belongings and approach *letting go with compassion and care*. For now, take some time to fine-tune your blueprint and begin where it makes sense for you. Remember, this isn't about getting it perfect—it's about creating progress that feels good and grounded.

Chapter Two

Navigating Emotional Attachments

A Compassionate Approach to Letting Go

Every cherished item in our home holds a story—fragments of our past, glimpses of who we were, and sometimes, dreams that never quite came to be. Our connection to these belongings often runs deeper than we realize. It's not just about the objects themselves—it's the memories they carry, the people they remind us of, and the roles they've played in shaping our lives.

Understanding these emotional ties isn't about judgment. It's about approaching them with compassion—acknowledging the meaning behind what we've kept, while gently making room for what's next. These attachments can form an intricate web of identity, memory, and relationship, which is why letting go can feel so deeply personal. But within that challenge is an opportunity—a chance to grow, to heal, and to move forward with greater clarity.

When we explore our attachments with curiosity rather than pressure, we give ourselves permission to honor what matters most, and to release what no longer serves our lives today. Letting go doesn't have to mean forgetting. It can mean finding new, meaningful ways to carry our stories forward.

I was reminded of this during a particularly tender downsizing project with Eleanor, a retired art teacher preparing to move from her longtime family home into a smaller apartment. The toughest part wasn't sorting through kitchen drawers or linen closets—it was stepping into her late husband's art studio, untouched since his passing three years earlier. Every brush, half-finished canvas, and paint-splattered apron carried weight and meaning.

Rather than rushing the process, I urged her to take her time. Together, we created a memory book—photographs of his most meaningful works and tools, paired with Eleanor's handwritten reflections. We chose a few treasured pieces for her new space and arranged to donate the rest of his high-quality supplies to a local art school's scholarship program. What started as a painful task became something far more powerful: a way to honor his legacy while opening space for the next chapter of her life.

Eleanor later told me that the process brought her closer to his memory—not by holding on to everything, but by thoughtfully choosing what to keep and how to let the rest carry forward into the lives of others. That experience reminded me of an important truth: *sometimes the most meaningful way to preserve the past is by creating something beautiful from it.*

As we move through this chapter, we'll look at practical ways to navigate these emotional layers with care. You'll learn how to honor your attachments while creating space for new experiences, new energy, and new beginnings. This part of the journey isn't just about what we let go. It's also about what we carry forward with intention.

As we delve deeper into this topic, you'll discover that addressing emotional attachments isn't about forcing yourself to let go or dismissing the significance of your possessions. Instead, it's about developing a more conscious relationship with your belongings, one that allows you to preserve what truly matters while releasing what might be holding you back from living more fully in the present.

Understanding the Psychology of Emotional Attachments to Objects

Our relationships with physical objects begin forming in early childhood, shaping how we interact with possessions throughout our lives. These attachments serve important psychological needs - from preserving precious memories and maintaining connections to loved ones, to reinforcing our sense of identity and security. Understanding these deep-rooted connections is crucial for approaching the downsizing process with self-awareness and compassion.

These emotional bonds often fall into distinct categories that influence how we relate to our possessions:

- **Security Objects:** Items that provide comfort and a sense of safety, like a favorite blanket or meaningful piece of jewelry

- **Identity Markers:** Possessions that reflect who we are or aspire to be, such as professional credentials or hobby equipment

- **Connection Objects:** Things that link us to important relationships or memories, like inherited items or gifts

- **Legacy Items:** Objects that represent our family history or personal achievements

- **Potential Objects:** Things we keep for their perceived future usefulness or value

Understanding which category our attachments fall into can help us make more mindful decisions about what to keep and what to let go. For example, recognizing that an old jacket represents a connection to a departed loved one rather than just being a piece of clothing allows us to explore alternative ways of preserving that connection while releasing the physical item.

When my friend Anne downsize her mother's home after she moved to assisted living, a collection of well-worn cookbooks initially seemed like obvious candidates for donation. However, as Anne flipped through their pages, she discovered handwritten notes in the margins - her mother's culinary secrets and memories of family meals. Rather than keeping all the books, we photographed the meaningful annotations and created a digital recipe collection that preserved these precious memories while allowing Anne to let go of the physical books.

The tendency to hold onto items often masks deeper emotional needs or unresolved feelings. We might cling to possessions out of anxiety about the future, grief over past losses, or a desire to maintain control. By approaching these attachments with curiosity rather than judgment, we can better understand our motivations and make more intentional choices about our possessions.

When helping with my elderly neighbor Tom during his downsizing journey, we discovered his reluctance to part with decades of work-related documents stemmed not from their practical value, but from uncertainty about his identity post-retirement. By acknowledging this underlying concern, we were able to focus on preserving select items that honored his career while creating space for his new chapter in life.

The key to navigating emotional attachments lies not in forcing ourselves to let go, but in developing a more conscious relationship with our possessions. This might mean:

- Taking time to reflect on why certain items hold such significance

- Exploring alternative ways to honor memories and connections

- Acknowledging the difference between the memory and the physical item

- Giving ourselves permission to keep truly meaningful items while releasing others

- Creating rituals or ceremonies for letting go of particularly significant objects

As we develop this understanding, we often find that our attachments to objects become less rigid and more fluid. We begin to see that our memories and relationships exist independently of physical items, and that letting go of excess possessions can actually create space for new experiences and connections to flourish.

This shift in perspective doesn't happen overnight, and it's perfectly normal to experience a range of emotions during the process. The goal isn't to become detached from our possessions, but rather to cultivate a healthier, more balanced relationship with them - one that enhances rather than hinders our well-being and personal growth.

Techniques for Processing Grief and Loss During Downsizing

The process of downsizing often triggers unexpected waves of grief and loss, particularly when sorting through items that connect us to important life transitions or departed loved ones. This emotional response is not only natural but deserves our gentle attention and care as we navigate the journey of letting go. Through helping three elderly couples downsize their homes and supporting friends through similar transitions, I've learned that acknowledging and processing these feelings is as crucial as the physical act of sorting and organizing.

When helping my friend Helen downsize her family home, I witnessed the profound importance of creating space for grief during this process. Each room held memories of her life with her children, making even simple decisions feel overwhelming. Together, we developed a gentle approach that allowed her to honor her emotions while still moving forward. We would begin each session by lighting a candle and taking a moment to acknowledge the memories and feelings that might surface. This simple ritual created a container for her grief while signaling that it was okay to proceed with the task at hand.

Here are several proven techniques for processing grief and loss during downsizing:

- Create a 'Pause Box' for emotionally charged items that need more time and reflection

- Establish regular 'Memory Breaks' during sorting sessions to share stories and honor feelings

- Practice mindful breathing when feeling overwhelmed by emotions

- Keep a downsizing journal to document memories and process feelings

- Set up a designated 'Memory Station' for photographing and documenting significant items

The key is to move at a pace that feels respectful to your emotional process while maintaining gentle forward momentum. Remember that grief during downsizing often comes in layers. You might feel sadness about letting go of an item itself, grief for the person or time period it represents, and anxiety about future changes. All of these feelings deserve space and acknowledgment. I encourage people to create a 'Memory Bridge' - identifying ways to honor the *essence* of what they're letting go of while moving forward. This might mean creating a photo album of cherished items before donating them, writing letters to capture associated memories, or finding new ways to honor traditions without keeping all the physical objects.

One particularly effective technique I've found is the 'Story Circle' method. Before letting go of emotionally significant items, gather with supportive friends or family members to share the stories these objects hold. This not only helps process grief but often reveals that the most valuable aspects of our possessions are the memories and connections they represent - elements we carry with us regardless of whether we keep the physical items.

The grieving process during downsizing also offers unexpected opportunities for healing and growth. By consciously engaging with our emotions rather than avoiding them, we often discover new layers of resilience and wisdom. I've witnessed countless individuals transform their relationship with loss through this process, finding that mindful downsizing can actually become a powerful tool for processing both past and present grief.

When working with emotional items, consider these gentle approaches:

- Set aside specific times for processing emotionally charged categories

- Create rituals for saying goodbye to significant items

- Document the stories and memories associated with important pieces

- Identify ways to honor the essence of what you're letting go

- Seek support from friends, family, or grief counselors when needed

Remember that there's no universal timeline for processing grief during downsizing. Some days you might move swiftly through decisions, while others require more pause and reflection. This variation is normal and deserves your compassion. The goal isn't to eliminate emotional attachment but to find healthy ways to honor our connections while creating space for new possibilities in our lives.

Creating Memory Preservation Strategies Without Keeping Everything

One of the most challenging aspects of downsizing is finding ways to honor our memories without keeping every physical item associated with them. Through my experiences helping family and friends navigate this delicate balance, I've discovered that the key lies in shifting our focus from preserving objects to preserving the essence of our memories in more meaningful and space-efficient ways.

I learned this lesson while helping my mother downsize her collection of family photographs and memorabilia. Together, we discovered that by digitizing selected photos and creating themed digital albums with recorded stories, we could actually engage with our family history more frequently and meaningfully than when everything was stored in boxes in the attic. This revelation transformed how I approach memory preservation with others who are downsizing.

Here are several effective strategies for preserving memories while minimizing physical items:

- Create digital memory books with photos and written stories

- Record video or audio narratives about significant items before letting them go

- Select one representative item from a collection to keep and document the rest

- Use high-quality photographs to capture detailed items before parting with them

- Create memory boxes with strict size limitations for physical keepsakes

The digital age has provided us with unprecedented opportunities to preserve memories and reduce physical clutter. One effective technique I've discovered is what I call the 'Memory Mapping Method.' This approach involves creating a digital or written narrative that captures the emotional significance of items before letting them go. For instance, when helping an elderly neighbor downsize her grandmother's china collection, we photographed each piece and recorded the stories behind them – which pieces were used for holiday meals, which were wedding gifts, and the special memories associated with family gatherings. This allowed her to keep the two most meaningful pieces while preserving the rich family history connected to the entire collection.

It's important to remember that our memories reside in our hearts and minds, not in physical objects. The items we keep should serve as touchstones to these memories rather than bearing the full weight of preserving them. Consider these guidelines when developing your memory preservation strategy:

- Focus on capturing the story or meaning behind items rather than keeping every physical representation

- Set clear criteria for what constitutes a 'memory keeper' versus a general memento

- Create organized digital archives that are easy to access and share with family

- Establish regular review periods to ensure your preservation methods remain relevant and meaningful

- Consider how future generations might want to engage with these memories

My co-worker David found particular success with what we called the 'Legacy Box' approach. Instead of keeping every item from his military service, he carefully selected one uniform, his medals, and a few significant photographs. He then created a detailed digital record of his service history, including scanned documents and recorded stories about his experiences. This concentrated collection proved far more meaningful than the scattered memorabilia he had previously maintained.

The process of preserving memories without keeping everything physical requires trust – trust that our memories will remain vivid even without every tangible reminder, and trust that by carefully curating what we keep, we actually enhance our connection to what matters most. Through thoughtful selection and creative documentation, we can honor our past while creating space for our present and future.

Remember that memory preservation is not about quantity but quality. By focusing on capturing the essence of our memories rather than maintaining every physical item associated with them, we create a more meaningful and sustainable way to honor our experiences and relationships. This approach not only frees up physical space but often leads to a deeper appreciation of the memories we choose to preserve.

Managing Family Expectations and Inherited Items

Managing family expectations during the downsizing process often feels like navigating an emotional maze, especially when dealing with inherited items that carry generations of memories and meaning. Through my experiences helping several families navigate these sensitive waters, I've learned that success lies not just in the physical sorting of items, but in the careful handling of relationships and emotions involved.

While helping the Anderson family manage their parents' estate, I witnessed firsthand how three siblings, each with different emotional attachments and expectations, needed to work through rooms full of family heirlooms and treasured possessions. What began as a potentially divisive situation transformed into a bonding experience through clear communication and structured decision-making processes.

Here are several essential strategies for managing family expectations around inherited items:

- Schedule regular family meetings to discuss the process and share concerns

- Create a fair system for distributing items that multiple family members want

- Document family stories and memories associated with significant pieces

- Establish clear timelines and deadlines for decision-making

- Develop a process for handling disagreements before they arise

One of the most effective approaches I've found is what I call the 'Heritage Circle' method. This involves gathering family members to share stories about significant items before any decisions about their fate are made. This process often reveals that what one person values about an object might be preserved in ways that don't require keeping the physical item.

For example, when my childhood friend's family struggled over their grandmother's extensive china collection, we discovered that what most members really valued were the memories of family dinners rather than the dishes themselves. This realization led to creative solutions - photographing the complete collection, selecting one place setting for each family member, and using the proceeds from selling the remainder to host a family reunion dinner that honored their grandmother's legacy of bringing the family together.

The key to managing inherited items lies in separating their emotional value from their physical presence. Consider these practical steps:

- Create a shared digital archive of family items with associated stories

- Establish clear criteria for what constitutes a 'must-keep' family heirloom

- Develop a rotation system for shared family treasures

- Find ways to honor family history without keeping every physical item

I often encourage families to use what I call the 'Legacy Lens' approach. This involves asking three essential questions about each inherited item:

1. Does this item actively contribute to honoring our family's legacy?

2. Is keeping this physical object the best way to preserve its associated memories?

3. Would the original owner want this item to be a source of burden or conflict?

These questions often help shift the conversation from 'who gets what' to 'how can we best honor our shared history?' Remember that managing family expectations isn't just about the items themselves - it's about maintaining and strengthening family bonds through the process. Sometimes, the most valuable inheritance isn't the physical items but the stories, values, and connections they represent.

Some families create 'Heritage Boxes'. Each family member receives a curated collection of smaller items, photographs, and documented stories that represent their connection to the family history. This way, everyone receives something meaningful while preventing the burden of excessive inherited items.

It's also crucial to acknowledge that different family members may have varying emotional attachments to items. What seems insignificant to one person might hold deep meaning for another. Creating space for these differences while maintaining forward momentum requires both compassion and clear boundaries.

When working with inherited items, consider these guidelines:

- Focus on preserving the essence of family history rather than every physical item

- Create systems for fairly distributing items when multiple people express interest

- Document the stories and memories associated with significant pieces

- Establish clear timelines for decision-making to prevent indefinite delays

- Find ways to honor family legacy through actions rather than just possessions

But managing family expectations and inherited items offers an opportunity to strengthen family bonds rather than strain them. By approaching these challenges with clarity, compassion, and creativity, we can actually transform what might be a source of conflict into a chance for deeper connection and shared purpose.

Self-Compassion Practices for the Letting-Go Process

The journey of letting-go requires both practical strategies and a gentle, understanding approach toward ourselves. Self-compassion isn't just helpful – it's essential for sustainable change and emotional well-being during this transformative journey.

I really came to understand this when I first tried to downsize my home. Each time I struggled to part with an item, I would berate With time and practice I can now acknowledge the difficulty of the process and extend the same kindness to ourselves that I would offer a dear friend facing similar challenges. Understanding that letting go of things is difficult and that it is ok to find it difficult, was a huge turning point for me.

Here are several foundational practices for cultivating self-compassion during the letting go process:

- Acknowledge the difficulty without judgment
- Practice gentle self-talk when facing challenging decisions
- Take mindful breaks when emotions feel overwhelming
- Celebrate small victories and progress
- Create personal rituals for processing difficult emotions

Before letting go of a challenging item, take a moment to express gratitude for what it has meant in your life, then consciously choose to release it with kindness – both to yourself and the item. This practice helps transform what might feel like loss into an act of intentional growth.

It's crucial to understand that attachment to possessions often runs deeper than the items themselves. They can represent hopes, dreams, relationships, and parts of our identity. Approaching these attachments with curiosity rather than criticism allows us to better understand ourselves and make more mindful choices about what we truly want to keep in our lives.

Consider incorporating these self-compassion practices into your downsizing journey:

- Start each sorting session with a moment of mindful breathing

- Keep a downsizing journal to process emotions and track progress

- Create a self-care toolkit for challenging moments

- Set realistic expectations and timelines

- Celebrate the courage it takes to let go

The practice of self-compassion during downsizing isn't about avoiding difficult emotions or decisions. Instead, it's about creating a supportive internal environment that allows us to face these challenges with courage and wisdom. By treating ourselves with kindness throughout this process, we not only make the journey more manageable but also lay the foundation for lasting positive change in our relationship with possessions and ourselves.

Transforming Emotional Attachments into Meaningful Actions

One of the most powerful ways to honor our emotional attachments while creating space in our lives is to transform these connections into meaningful actions. When we shift our focus from keeping physical items to embodying the values and memories they represent, we often find deeper satisfaction and more authentic ways to preserve what matters most.

I experienced this transformation firsthand while helping an elderly neighbor sort through decades of teaching materials. Rather than keeping every lesson plan and student project, we created what we called an 'Education Legacy Project.' She selected key items to donate to new teachers, started mentoring at a local school, and created a digital archive of her most innovative teaching methods to share with others. This approach allowed her to honor her teaching career while transforming her attachment to physical items into meaningful contributions to her community.

The process of transforming attachments into actions involves several key steps:

- Identify the core values or memories represented by meaningful items

- Explore ways to actively honor these values in your daily life

- Create new traditions that capture the essence of what you're preserving

- Find opportunities to share the wisdom or joy these items represent

- Develop projects or initiatives that extend the legacy of significant possessions

This approach is particularly powerful when dealing with inherited items or collections that hold deep emotional significance. While helping Thomas process his grandfather's extensive woodworking tools, we developed a plan that transformed his attachment into purpose. Instead of keeping tools he rarely used, he donated most of them to a youth vocational program while keeping just a few special pieces. He then began teaching basic woodworking skills to neighborhood children, sharing not just techniques but the values of craftsmanship and patience his grandfather had instilled in him.

The key is to recognize that our attachments often represent deeper values, skills, or connections that can be expressed and shared in multiple ways. Consider these questions when exploring how to transform your attachments:

- What core values does this item or collection represent?

- How can I actively embody these values in my life?

- What wisdom or joy from this item could benefit others?

- What new traditions could I create that honor these memories?

- How might sharing these stories or skills enrich my community?

One particularly effective method I've found is the 'Legacy in Action' framework. This approach helps identify specific ways to transform attachments into meaningful projects or practices. For instance, when helping Emma process her mother's extensive garden tool collection, we didn't just focus on deciding what to keep or discard. Instead, we explored how she could honor her mother's love of gardening through action. She ultimately created a community garden program, teaching others the skills her mother had taught her while using just a carefully chosen selection of her mother's most essential tools.

This transformation of attachments into actions can take many forms:

- Converting collections into educational resources
- Using inherited skills to mentor others
- Creating community projects that extend family traditions
- Developing new rituals that honor old memories
- Finding ways to share stories and wisdom with future generations

The beauty of this approach lies in its ability to free us from the burden of physical possessions while amplifying the impact of what we truly value. When we transform our attachments into actions, we often find that the memories and connections we sought to preserve become more vibrant and meaningful than when they were tied to physical items alone.

Remember that this transformation doesn't mean completely letting go of all physical reminders. Instead, it's about finding a balance where carefully chosen items serve as touchstones for active practices and meaningful engagement with what we value most. Through this process, we often discover that our legacy lives not in the things we keep, but in the actions we take and the lives we touch.

As you consider how to transform your own attachments into meaningful actions, start small. Choose one significant item or collection and explore how its deeper meaning could be expressed through action. You might be surprised to find that what began as a process of letting go becomes an opportunity for growth, connection, and positive impact in ways you never imagined.As we conclude this chapter on navigating emotional attachments, we return to Eleanor's story – her journey of transforming her late husband's art studio from a space frozen in time to a legacy that continues to inspire others. Her experience reminds us that addressing our emotional attachments to possessions isn't just about deciding what to keep or discard; it's about understanding the deeper connections these items represent and finding meaningful ways to honor them.

Throughout this chapter, we've explored various dimensions of emotional attachment and discovered practical strategies for moving forward. From understanding the psychology behind our connections to objects to developing compassionate approaches for letting go, we've seen how acknowledging our emotions while taking mindful action can transform the downsizing process from one of loss to one of liberation.

The journey of navigating emotional attachments teaches us several key lessons:

- Our memories and relationships exist independently of physical objects
- We can honor our past while creating space for our future

- Self-compassion is essential for sustainable change

- Creative preservation methods can help us maintain what matters most

- Transforming attachments into meaningful actions deepens their significance

As you move forward with your own downsizing journey, remember that there's no universal timeline for processing emotional attachments. Some decisions will come easily, while others may require more time and reflection. What matters most is maintaining a balance between honoring your feelings and moving forward with intention.

When helping my friend Maria downsize her mother's home, we discovered that her strongest attachments weren't to the valuable items, but to simple everyday objects that held precious memories of shared moments. Together, we found ways to honor these connections through photographs, stories, and new traditions, proving that the essence of our memories can live on even as we let go of physical reminders.

As we close this chapter, I encourage you to continue approaching your emotional attachments with both curiosity and kindness. Letting go of physical items doesn't mean letting go of the memories, relationships, or values they represent. In fact, it often creates space for those connections to be honored in new and meaningful ways—ways that feel lighter, more intentional, and more in tune with the life you're living now.

In the next chapter, we'll explore creative, thoughtful ways to preserve your most meaningful memories—without feeling the need to keep everything. You'll learn practical techniques for documenting, digitizing, and reimagining keepsakes in formats that add beauty and meaning to your life rather than weighing it down.

Your relationship with your possessions is deeply personal, and this part of the journey can bring up a wide range of emotions. But you're not walking it alone. The insights and tools we've explored here are meant to support you as you make decisions that reflect your values, your memories, and your vision for what comes next. With each small, intentional step, you're not just letting go—you're creating space for what truly matters to stay with you in a way that feels just right.

Chapter Three

The Sentimental Items Solution

Creative Ways to Preserve Memories

The box filled with your child's artwork. Your grandmother's delicate china collection. The souvenirs gathered from faraway adventures. These aren't just things—they're vessels of memory, woven into the story of your life. They carry moments, milestones, and pieces of the people and places that have shaped you.

As we move through the process of downsizing, one of the most tender challenges we face is learning how to honor those memories without feeling the need to hold on to every physical reminder. It's not about discarding what matters—it's about curating what matters most, in a way that supports your life today.

Throughout our lives, we gather tangible keepsakes that represent love, achievement, and meaningful moments. These objects often become emotional anchors, making it understandably difficult to let them go. But in this digital age, we have new, creative ways to preserve and celebrate those memories—without needing to keep every single item.

The key is in gently shifting our perspective. Our memories don't live in the objects themselves—they live within us. And when we learn to separate the memory from the item, we give ourselves permission to hold on in new ways—ways that feel lighter, more intentional, and often even more meaningful.

These emotional crossroads often surface during big transitions—moving to a smaller space, helping aging parents relocate, or simply deciding it's time to make more room in your current environment. These are the moments that ask us to rethink our relationship with sentimental items—and invite us to create space not just in our homes, but in our hearts.

While helping an elderly couple downsize their home of forty years, I encountered a situation that perfectly illustrates the power of creative memory preservation. Miriam had kept every greeting card she'd received since her wedding day, filling multiple boxes that she couldn't bear to part with. Together, we explored a solution that honored these precious memories while significantly reducing physical space. We spent an afternoon photographing the most special cards, recording Miriam's stories about each one, and creating a beautiful digital memory book with her favorite messages and signatures. For the handful of most precious cards – her husband's first Valentine to her, her children's handmade Mother's Day cards – we created a small shadow box display. The rest we ceremonially recycled after Miriam had captured their essence digitally.

What started as twelve boxes of cards became one cherished display piece and a digital album that Miriam could easily share with her family. The process helped her realize that the memories lived in her heart, not in the physical cards, and she felt lighter having found a way to honor these remembrances without being burdened by their physical presence. This experience showed how we can preserve what matters most without keeping everything.

In this chapter, we'll explore innovative solutions for preserving your most precious memories while reducing physical clutter. You'll discover practical strategies for digitizing important documents, creating meaningful displays, and thoughtfully curating emotional keepsakes. Most importantly, you'll learn to distinguish between the memory itself and the physical item that triggers it, empowering you to make confident decisions about what to keep, what to digitize, and what to let go - all while honoring the emotional significance of your possessions.

Digital Memory Preservation Techniques and Tools

In today's digital world, we have powerful tools at our fingertips to preserve our cherished memories without keeping every physical item. When I first began helping my friend Emma explore digital preservation methods for her family photos, she was hesitant to trust technology with her precious memories. However, after we created her first digital memory album, she was amazed by how much more she engaged with these memories when they were organized and readily available on her tablet.

The foundation of digital preservation starts with high-quality scanning or photography of your items. For photographs and documents, a good flatbed scanner can capture crisp, detailed images that often look better than the originals, especially if they've aged or faded. For three-dimensional objects like trophies, artwork, or cherished toys, use a digital camera or smartphone in natural lighting to capture multiple angles. Remember to set your devices to the highest quality settings - storage is relatively inexpensive compared to the value of preserving these memories in the best possible way.

Here are the essential tools for creating your digital memory archive:

- Cloud storage services for secure backup (like Google Drive, iCloud, or Dropbox)

- A quality scanner or smartphone with a good camera

- External hard drive for local backup

- Photo organization software for cataloging and editing

- Digital diary or journaling app for recording stories and memories

The key to successful digital preservation lies not just in capturing images, but in organizing them meaningfully. Create a clear folder structure with categories that make sense to you - perhaps by year, event type, or family member. Add descriptive file names and tags that will help you locate specific memories later. I always encourage people to include written context with their digital archives - the stories behind the photos, the significance of certain items, and the memories they evoke.

One of the most powerful aspects of digital preservation is the ability to share memories easily with family members. When my neighbor Robert digitized his father's war memorabilia, we created a shared digital album that allowed his siblings across the country to view and contribute their own memories and stories. This collaborative approach often reveals new layers of meaning and connection that might have remained hidden if the physical items had stayed in a box in one person's attic.

Remember to implement a reliable backup system for your digital memories. I recommend following the 3-2-1 rule: maintain three copies of your important files, store them on at least two different types of media, and keep one copy off-site or in the cloud. This approach ensures that your precious memories remain safe even if technology fails or natural disasters strike.

Consider creating themed digital collections that tell specific stories or capture particular aspects of your life. For instance, you might compile a digital recipe book with photos of family recipes written in loved ones' handwriting, or create a virtual museum of your children's artwork complete with the stories behind each masterpiece. These curated collections often prove more meaningful than keeping every physical item, as they focus on the essence of what makes these memories special.

When digitizing sentimental items, take time to record the stories and emotions connected to them. Use your smartphone's voice recorder to capture your narratives, or type them directly into notes attached to the digital files. These personal annotations transform simple images into rich, multi-layered memories that future generations can truly appreciate and understand.

Creating Memory Books and Time Capsules

Memory books and time capsules offer powerful ways to preserve cherished memories while significantly reducing physical clutter. When I helped my friend Jennifer organize her children's school memorabilia, she discovered that creating a dedicated memory book actually helped her feel more connected to these treasured moments than when they were scattered across multiple storage containers.

Creating a memory book begins with thoughtful curation. Start by gathering your sentimental items and sorting them into themes or time periods. This might include photographs, letters, certificates, ticket stubs, or small flat mementos. The key is to select items that truly capture the spirit of the memories you want to preserve. Remember, you're not trying to keep everything – you're creating a curated collection that tells your story.

Here are essential supplies for creating your memory book:

- An acid-free album or scrapbook
- Archival-quality page protectors
- Acid-free adhesive or photo corners
- Archival-quality pens for journaling

- Small envelopes or pockets for delicate items

- Clear labels for dating and describing items

The process of creating a memory book should be treated as a meaningful ritual rather than a rushed task. Set aside dedicated time to work on your book, perhaps playing music from the era you're documenting or sharing stories with family members as you work. This approach transforms the preservation process into a memory-making activity itself.

Time capsules offer another creative approach to preserving memories while downsizing. Unlike traditional time capsules that are buried and opened years later, modern memory capsules can be created as accessible archives that represent specific periods or milestones in your life. Last year, I helped a friend create what we called a 'Decade Capsule' – a beautifully crafted box containing carefully chosen items representing his children's first ten years, including a favorite toy, a handwritten letter from each year, and an annual family photo.

When creating a time capsule, consider these guidelines:

- Choose a high-quality, acid-free container that will protect items long-term

- Include a detailed inventory of contents with dates and descriptions

- Add context through written narratives or recorded stories

- Select items that truly represent the time period or theme

- Consider including current events or cultural references for historical context

One of the most powerful aspects of both memory books and time capsules is their ability to transform large collections of memorabilia into compact, meaningful archives. While helping my friend Sarah downsize her travel souvenirs from twenty years of adventures, we created a beautiful travel memory book that actually told the story of her journeys more effectively than the scattered collection of items ever did.

Remember to include written context with both memory books and time capsules. Future generations will appreciate understanding why certain items were significant enough to preserve. Take time to record the stories, emotions, and circumstances surrounding each item. This documentation often becomes more valuable than the physical items themselves.

Consider creating themed memory books or capsules for different aspects of life: childhood memories, family traditions, career milestones, or special hobbies. This organized approach makes it easier to share specific memories with different family members and helps prevent the overwhelming feeling of trying to preserve everything in one place.

The beauty of memory books and time capsules lies in their ability to transform the downsizing process from one of loss to one of intentional curation. By thoughtfully selecting and preserving items that truly matter, we often find that we connect more deeply with our memories than when they were buried in boxes or drawers. These carefully crafted archives become treasured family heirlooms that take up minimal space while maximizing meaning.

The Art of Photographing Sentimental Items

Photographing sentimental items is both an art and a practical skill that can dramatically ease the emotional burden of downsizing. When I first started photographing our family heirlooms, I discovered that the process itself often became a meaningful ritual of remembrance and release. Through the lens of a camera, we can capture not just the physical appearance of an item, but also its essence and the memories it represents.

The key to successfully photographing sentimental items lies in preparation and attention to detail. Before beginning, gather your materials: a camera or smartphone with a good quality camera, proper lighting (natural light works best), a clean, neutral background, and any props or supports needed to display items effectively. I always set up a small photography station near a window, where natural light can illuminate objects without harsh shadows or glare.

Here are essential techniques for capturing sentimental items:

- Use a neutral background (white, gray, or black) to make items stand out

- Position items near a window for natural lighting, avoiding direct sunlight

- Capture multiple angles to show dimension and detail

- Include close-up shots of special features or markings

- Take context shots showing the item's size or scale

- Photograph any labels, marks, or inscriptions separately

One of my most meaningful experiences was photographing my grandmother's collection of hand-embroidered linens. Instead of keeping dozens of delicate tablecloths and napkins that were slowly yellowing in storage, I created a beautiful photo series that captured the intricate details of each pattern. I photographed the items laid flat to show the full designs, then took close-ups of the most detailed sections and any special stitching techniques she had used. The resulting digital archive actually allowed me to appreciate her craftsmanship more than when the linens were packed away in boxes.

When photographing three-dimensional objects, consider creating a visual story through multiple images. For example, when documenting a child's favorite toy, capture it from different angles, include close-ups of worn areas that show how well-loved it was, and perhaps take a photo of it in its familiar spot in the child's room. These different perspectives help preserve not just the object's appearance, but its role in your life.

Lighting plays a crucial role in capturing sentimental items effectively. Position your photography station near a window where indirect natural light can illuminate your items evenly. Avoid using flash, as it can create harsh reflections and wash out details. If you're working in a dimly lit space, consider using a simple desk lamp with a daylight bulb, positioning it at an angle to minimize shadows.

After capturing your images, take time to organize them meaningfully. Create clear file names that include the item's description and any relevant dates or details. Consider adding written descriptions or voice recordings that explain the significance of each item. These notes transform simple photographs into rich historical documents for future generations.

Remember that the goal isn't just to create a visual inventory, but to capture the essence of what makes each item special. Sometimes this means photographing objects in context - a beloved book open to a favorite passage, a cherished piece of jewelry being worn, or a family heirloom in use during a holiday celebration. These contextual photographs often evoke memories more powerfully than simple documentary-style shots.

The process of photographing sentimental items often becomes a therapeutic exercise in itself. As you handle each object, take time to recall its stories and significance. Many people find that this mindful documentation process helps them feel more comfortable letting go of physical items, knowing they've preserved their essence in a meaningful way.

Repurposing and Upcycling Emotional Keepsakes

Transforming sentimental items into functional or decorative pieces offers a beautiful way to honor memories while creating something new and meaningful for your current life. When I downsized my grandmother's collection of vintage teacups, I discovered that repurposing these precious items allowed me to keep their essence while giving them new purpose - several became charming succulent planters for my kitchen windowsill, creating a living tribute to her love of gardening and afternoon tea rituals.

Repurposing sentimental items requires a balance of creativity and respect for the original piece. Before beginning any project, consider the item's condition, its emotional significance, and how you might incorporate it into your current lifestyle. Sometimes the most meaningful transformations maintain elements of the item's original purpose while adapting it for contemporary use.

Here are creative ways to repurpose common sentimental items:

- Transform children's artwork into custom fabric patterns for pillows or quilts

- Create jewelry from broken china or beloved ceramic pieces

- Convert vintage clothing into decorative throw pillows or wall hangings

- Use old letters or cards to create framed collages or decoupage projects

- Repurpose family heirlooms into functional household items

One of my most meaningful projects involved transforming my father's collection of well-worn flannel shirts into a cozy throw blanket. Each square of fabric held memories of fishing trips and weekend projects, and the finished blanket became both a functional item and a tactile connection to those cherished moments. The process of creating something new from these meaningful materials often becomes its own form of therapeutic closure.

When approaching an upcycling project, consider how the transformed item will fit into your current lifestyle. The goal is to create something that honors the original memory while serving a practical or aesthetic purpose in your present life. This might mean turning a grandfather's old toolbox into a unique bathroom organizer or converting vintage costume jewelry into decorative picture frames.

Document your transformation projects through photographs and written descriptions. Capture images of the original items, the creation process, and the final result. These records become part of the item's ongoing story, adding new layers of meaning to already precious possessions. Include notes about your creative decisions and how the transformed piece connects to your memories of the original item.

Remember that not every sentimental item needs to be physically transformed to be honored. Sometimes simply displaying a small portion of a larger collection can be enough. For instance, when I helped my mother downsize her extensive teapot collection, we selected a single piece to transform into a unique succulent garden centerpiece, allowing her to let go of the rest while maintaining a meaningful connection to the memory.

When working with family heirlooms or shared sentimental items, communicate with family members about your plans for repurposing. Sometimes siblings or relatives might want to participate in the transformation process or share ideas about how to honor the item's memory. These collaborative projects can strengthen family bonds while creating new shared memories.

The key to successful repurposing lies in maintaining a balance between honoring the past and creating something useful for the present. Focus on projects that feel authentic to both the original item's significance and your current needs. This mindful approach helps ensure that your transformed pieces become treasured elements of your daily life rather than just different forms of clutter.

Setting Boundaries with Inherited Family Heirlooms

Inherited family heirlooms often carry the weight of both memories and expectations, making them particularly challenging to address during the downsizing process. Through helping families navigate these sensitive situations, I've learned that establishing clear boundaries isn't just about the physical items – it's about managing emotions, family dynamics, and sometimes generations of accumulated expectations.

When helping the Anderson family downsize their mother's home, I witnessed firsthand how three siblings struggled with their extensive collection of antique furniture and china that had been passed down through four generations. Each piece came with its own story and an unspoken obligation to preserve it for future generations. The turning point came when they sat down together and openly discussed what these items truly meant to each family member, leading to an important realization: honoring family history doesn't require keeping every physical item.

Here are essential strategies for setting healthy boundaries with family heirlooms:

- Establish clear criteria for what you'll keep based on both practical considerations and emotional significance

- Create a family communication plan before making decisions about shared heirlooms

- Set realistic limits on storage space dedicated to inherited items

- Document items' histories before letting them go

- Consider rotating seasonal or holiday items among family members

The key to successfully managing inherited items lies in open communication and establishing clear parameters early in the process. Start by having honest conversations with family members about expectations and limitations. It's perfectly acceptable to say, "I can only accommodate a few pieces that truly speak to me and fit my lifestyle." This transparency helps prevent misunderstandings and hurt feelings later.

When working with inherited items, consider creating what I call a "Heritage Impact Scale." This involves rating each item on both its practical utility and its emotional significance. Items that score high in both categories are natural keepers, while those with lower scores might be better honored through photographs or by passing them to other family members who can better appreciate and use them.

One particularly effective approach is the "Family Heirloom Rotation System." Rather than one person feeling obligated to store and maintain all family heirlooms, items are shared among family members who each keep them for an agreed-upon period. This approach allows everyone to enjoy special pieces while sharing the responsibility of preservation.

Remember that saying no to inherited items doesn't mean rejecting your family history or memories. Recently, I helped a friend photograph and document her grandmother's extensive collection of Depression glass before selecting just a few key pieces to keep. The rest were thoughtfully distributed among family members or sold to collectors who would appreciate them. This process allowed her to honor her grandmother's memory while maintaining boundaries about what she could reasonably accommodate in her home.

It's also important to recognize that future generations may have different relationships with physical objects than previous ones. When helping families downsize, I often encourage them to think about the burden they might be placing on their children by preserving too many heirlooms. Consider creating a digital archive of family treasures, complete with stories and photographs, which can be shared with future generations without requiring physical storage space.

Setting boundaries with inherited items often requires us to challenge long-held family narratives about obligation and preservation. Remember that your role is to be a thoughtful curator of family history, not its warehouse. By establishing clear boundaries and communicating them with compassion, you can honor your family's legacy while maintaining a space that serves your current needs and lifestyle.

Establishing Personal Guidelines for Sentimental Items

Creating personal guidelines for sentimental items is essential for maintaining a balanced approach to preserving memories while avoiding clutter. Through my experiences helping family and friends navigate this delicate process, I've discovered that having clear, personalized criteria makes decision-making significantly easier and more consistent. When I helped my friend Rebecca develop her guidelines, she transformed from someone who kept every birthday card to a person who could confidently decide which items truly deserved space in her life.

The key to establishing effective guidelines is creating a framework that reflects your values, space limitations, and emotional needs. Start by asking yourself these fundamental questions: What types of items consistently bring you joy when you see or use them? Which memories feel most important to preserve physically rather than digitally? How much space can you realistically dedicate to sentimental items?

Here are foundational elements to consider when creating your personal guidelines:

- Set specific limits for different categories of sentimental items

- Define criteria for what makes an item truly meaningful

- Establish a regular review schedule for sentimental collections

- Create rules for new sentimental items entering your space

- Determine which types of items can be digitized versus kept physically

One of the most effective approaches I've found is the "Memory Value Assessment." This involves rating sentimental items on three key factors: emotional significance, practical use, and physical condition. Items scoring high in all three areas are natural keepers, while others might be better honored through photographs or stories.

When working with my neighbor Lisa, a young mother overwhelmed by her children's artwork and school projects, we created what we called the 'Seasonal Rotation System.' Instead of keeping every piece, she selected the most meaningful items from each season to display, photographed the rest, and created digital albums organized by school year. This system allowed her to honor her children's creativity while maintaining manageable physical archives.

Your guidelines should include clear parameters for different types of sentimental items. For instance, you might decide to keep one representative piece from each family member's china collection rather than entire sets, or limit yourself to a single memory box for each decade of your life. The key is creating boundaries that feel both respectful to the memories and sustainable for your lifestyle.

Remember to build flexibility into your guidelines while maintaining clear limits. Life events, moves, or changes in living situations might require adjusting your criteria, but having a basic framework helps prevent emotional decision-making from leading to clutter accumulation. I always encourage reviewing and refining guidelines annually, ensuring they continue to serve evolving needs.

One particularly effective guideline to develop is the 'One In, One Out' rule for sentimental items. When a new meaningful item enters your collection, review existing items to determine if something can be honored differently – perhaps through photography or by passing it along to another family member who might appreciate it more.

Your guidelines should also address how to handle unexpected sentimental items that surface during decluttering. Having predetermined criteria helps you make consistent decisions even when emotions are running high. For instance, you might decide that any newly discovered photographs will be digitized unless they're one-of-a-kind family portraits, or that cards will be kept for one year before being reviewed for long-term keeping.

Incorporate regular maintenance into your guidelines to prevent sentimental collections from growing unwieldy. Schedule periodic reviews – perhaps during significant life transitions or at the start of each year – to ensure your sentimental items continue to reflect what's truly meaningful in your life. This proactive approach helps prevent the guilt and overwhelm that often accompany large-scale decluttering projects.

Remember that your guidelines should reflect your personal values and living situation while remaining practical and sustainable. The goal isn't to eliminate sentimental items from your life but to create intentional space for those that truly matter. By establishing and following clear guidelines, you can maintain a meaningful collection of memories without letting it overwhelm your space or peace of mind.As we conclude our exploration of preserving memories while simplifying our lives, remember that the journey of managing sentimental items is deeply personal yet universally challenging. Throughout this chapter, we've discovered that our most precious memories don't reside in physical objects but in our hearts and stories. By embracing creative preservation techniques, from digital archives to thoughtfully curated memory books, we can honor our past while creating space for our present and future.

Miriam's experience with her greeting card collection perfectly illustrates the liberating power of intentional memory preservation. By thoughtfully documenting her cards while creating a beautiful display for select pieces, she discovered that memories become more accessible and meaningful when freed from the burden of physical clutter. Her story demonstrates that we can maintain deep connections to our past without being anchored by every physical reminder.

As you move forward with your own sentimental items, remember that letting go doesn't mean forgetting. Instead, it opens up new possibilities for engaging with and sharing your precious memories. Whether through creating digital archives, crafting memory books, or thoughtfully photographing cherished possessions, you now have the tools to preserve what matters most while lightening your physical load.

As you move forward with your own sentimental items, remember: letting go doesn't mean forgetting. It simply opens the door to new ways of honoring and sharing the memories you hold dear. Whether you're creating a digital archive, putting together a memory book, or thoughtfully photographing special items, you now have meaningful tools to preserve what matters most—without the weight of keeping everything.

The strategies we've explored—setting gentle boundaries with inherited heirlooms, creating personal guidelines for what to keep, and finding creative ways to preserve stories—are all part of a thoughtful process. This isn't about erasing your history; it's about curating it in a way that feels intentional and supportive of the life you're living now.

More than anything, we've discovered that memory preservation is about quality, not quantity. When we focus on the pieces that truly reflect our most meaningful experiences and relationships, we not only lighten our physical load—we also make more space for presence, connection, and new memories to come.

As you apply these ideas to your own keepsakes, be gentle with yourself. Take your time. Let the process unfold at a pace that feels right. This isn't about removing sentiment from your life—it's about creating a thoughtful, meaningful collection that brings comfort, beauty, and joy into your everyday space.

In the next chapter, we'll look at another layer of the downsizing journey: navigating the sometimes tricky family dynamics that can come with this process. We'll build on the foundation of mindful decision-making you've started here, and explore how to approach those conversations with clarity, care, and confidence.

For now, trust that your memories live within you—not in your closets or your boxes—and that letting go of objects can often help you feel even more connected to what truly matters.

Chapter Four

Family Dynamics and Downsizing

Managing Relationships Through Change

Family downsizing projects often reveal more than extra furniture and boxes of keepsakes—they tend to uncover the deeper layers of family history, emotion, and relationship dynamics that may have been quietly simmering for years. These transitions can bring their fair share of challenges, but they also offer powerful opportunities for healing, connection, and shared understanding.

Like a delicate dance, managing these moments well requires patience, empathy, and clear communication. Downsizing within families isn't just about sorting through belongings—it's about acknowledging the stories, expectations, and emotions attached to them. Each item often represents something more: a memory, a role, a relationship. And each family member brings their own perspective, emotional attachment, and approach to decision-making, which can make the process feel a little more complicated than expected.

Whether you're supporting aging parents as they transition to a smaller home, collaborating with siblings to sort through inherited items, or trying to set healthy boundaries around family possessions, understanding the dynamics at play can make all the difference. It's not just about logistics—it's about navigating personalities, emotions, and sometimes long-held family patterns with care and compassion.

Through my own work with several families—and particularly while helping my own elderly parents and in-laws move into new housing—I've seen how downsizing can be both a challenge and a turning point. What started as a logistical task can turn into something more meaningful: heartfelt conversations, shared laughter over old memories, and even unexpected moments of healing. I've learned that success in family downsizing isn't about how quickly decisions get made—it's about how respectfully and thoughtfully those decisions are approached.

In this chapter, we'll dive into practical strategies for navigating the sometimes delicate terrain of family dynamics during the downsizing process. You'll discover ways to communicate more clearly, approach differing perspectives with empathy, and create decision-making systems that feel fair and respectful to everyone involved. When handled with care, this process can do more than just clear space—it can open the door to deeper connection and understanding within your family.

I remember one family I knew who needed to sort through their late father's workshop. What began as a tense discussion about who would keep which tools quickly shifted into something more meaningful. By creating space for open conversations—and establishing regular family meetings to guide the process—they turned what could have been a source of conflict into a shared opportunity to remember, reflect, and honor their father's legacy. The downsizing process became a series of heartfelt gatherings where stories were exchanged, laughter resurfaced, and relationships quietly healed.

Together, we'll explore practical tools to help you manage common challenges—like navigating differing levels of emotional attachment, balancing conflicting priorities, and working through the sometimes heavy emotions tied to inherited belongings. You'll learn how to facilitate respectful conversations, establish clear roles, and move through the process in a way that preserves both your space and your relationships.

Remember, every family's downsizing journey is unique, shaped by their history, relationships, and current circumstances. The key is finding approaches that honor these individual dynamics while keeping the process moving forward constructively. As we delve into various strategies and solutions, consider how you might adapt them to suit your family's specific needs and situation.

Facilitating Productive Family Discussions About Downsizing

One of the most crucial elements in any family downsizing project is establishing open, respectful communication from the very beginning. The tone set in these initial conversations often determines how smoothly the entire process will unfold. The key lies in creating a safe space where every family member feels heard and valued, even when opinions differ.

Before diving into the practical aspects of downsizing, it's essential to lay some groundwork for productive discussions. I've found that choosing the right time and setting makes a significant difference - avoid times of high stress or when family members feel rushed. Consider scheduling a dedicated family meeting in a comfortable, neutral space where everyone can focus on the conversation without distractions.

Several fundamental elements help create successful family discussions about downsizing:

- Set clear expectations for the discussion

- Establish basic communication ground rules

- Create an agenda to keep conversations focused

- Ensure everyone has an opportunity to speak

- Take notes on decisions and action items

When my friend Maria's family needed to discuss downsizing their grandmother's home, we started with what I call a 'Memory Circle.' Each family member shared their favorite memory connected to the house, creating an atmosphere of appreciation rather than tension. This simple exercise helped everyone recognize that while they might disagree on specific items, they shared a common goal of honoring their family's history while moving forward.

A structured approach I've found particularly effective is the 'Three-Round Method' for family discussions about downsizing. The first round focuses solely on sharing feelings and concerns without making any decisions. The second round involves brainstorming possible solutions and approaches. The final round is dedicated to making concrete plans and assigning responsibilities. This systematic approach helps prevent emotional overwhelm and ensures that practical decisions incorporate everyone's input.

When engaging in these discussions, several communication strategies prove consistently helpful:

- Use 'I' statements when expressing feelings or concerns

- Practice active listening without interrupting

- Acknowledge emotions without judgment

- Focus on finding solutions rather than assigning blame

- Document agreements and decisions in writing

It's crucial to recognize that family members may have different communication styles and comfort levels with change. Some might prefer to process decisions slowly, while others want to move quickly. In helping the Anderson family downsize their home of thirty years, I saw how creating a balanced approach that respected these differences was essential for maintaining family harmony throughout the process.

When emotions run high, as they often do during downsizing discussions, structured breaks or 'pause points' can be invaluable. These brief intermissions allow everyone to step back, process their feelings, and return to the conversation with renewed perspective. Encourage family members to agree on a signal or phrase that anyone can use when they need a moment to regroup.

Remember that productive family discussions about downsizing aren't just about reaching decisions - they're about strengthening family bonds through shared understanding and respect. By approaching these conversations with patience, empathy, and clear structure, you can transform potentially challenging interactions into opportunities for deeper connection and mutual support.

To maintain momentum throughout the process, consider implementing these ongoing communication strategies:

- Schedule regular check-ins throughout the process
- Celebrate small victories and progress together
- Keep lines of communication open between meetings
- Be willing to adjust approaches based on family feedback
- Document and share progress to maintain momentum

Creating a shared digital space where family members can contribute thoughts, concerns, and ideas between face-to-face discussions often proves invaluable. This might be a private family group chat, shared document, or dedicated email thread. This ongoing connection helps maintain momentum and allows for thoughtful reflection between more formal discussions.

Through my experiences helping friends and family with numerous downsizing projects, I've observed that the most successful outcomes occur when communication remains consistent and respectful throughout the entire process. Even when disagreements arise, maintaining a foundation of open dialogue and mutual respect helps families navigate challenges while preserving and often strengthening their relationships.

Resolving Conflicts Over Shared and Inherited Items

The emotional complexity of shared and inherited items often creates unique challenges during the downsizing process. When multiple family members have connections to the same possessions, finding equitable and peaceful resolutions requires careful consideration of both practical and emotional factors.

I witnessed this firsthand when helping the Thompson family navigate the distribution of their mother's extensive collection of holiday decorations. Each sibling had strong emotional attachments to specific pieces, connected to different childhood memories. Rather than allowing these cherished items to become a source of conflict, we implemented what I call the 'Heritage Circle' approach

- gathering together to share stories and memories about different pieces before making any decisions about their distribution.

When approaching shared and inherited items, several key strategies can help maintain family harmony:

- Create a detailed inventory with photos and descriptions
- Document any existing promises or agreements
- Establish clear criteria for fair distribution
- Consider rotating possession of significant items
- Explore ways to share or duplicate meaningful objects

The power of storytelling in resolving conflicts over inherited items cannot be overstated. At its heart, our attachment to inherited possessions often stems from the memories and family history they represent. I saw this clearly when helping two sisters process their grandmother's china collection. By spending time sharing memories of holiday meals and special occasions, they realized that preserving the stories was more meaningful than keeping every physical piece.

Sometimes, the most effective solutions involve thinking creatively about how to honor shared heritage without keeping every item. I remember how the Weber family transformed their conflict over their father's beloved book collection by creating individual memory books containing photographs and descriptions of favorite volumes, along with handwritten stories about why each book held special meaning. This allowed them to preserve the essence of their father's passion while donating the physical books to a local library.

In cases where monetary value adds another layer of complexity, separating emotional and financial considerations often helps clarify decision-making. Consider these approaches:

- Obtain professional appraisals for valuable items

- Explore creative compromises like sharing or taking turns

- Document all final decisions in writing

- Create a fair process for future inherited items

- Plan ahead for long-term preservation

The 'Round Robin' method often proves particularly effective for distributing inherited items fairly. Family members take turns selecting items in a predetermined order, with the order reversing each round to ensure fairness. This systematic approach helps prevent simultaneous claims while giving everyone an opportunity to choose items that matter most to them.

One of the most valuable lessons I've learned through helping others with shared inheritances is the importance of implementing a 'cooling off' period when emotions run high. This pause in decision-making allows family members to process their feelings and often leads to more thoughtful, less reactive choices. During this time, contested items can be safely stored while family members focus on maintaining healthy relationships.

Remember that resolving conflicts over shared and inherited items isn't solely about dividing possessions - it's about preserving family bonds and honoring shared heritage. Some of the most successful resolutions come when families shift their focus from 'who gets what' to 'how can we best honor our shared memories and relationships.'

Creative solutions often emerge when families remain open to unconventional approaches. I've seen families successfully share custody of meaningful items, create high-quality reproductions, or transform objects into new forms that can be shared among multiple family members. The key lies in remaining flexible and focused on finding solutions that honor both the items' significance and family relationships.

In situations where complete agreement seems impossible, professional mediation can provide valuable neutral guidance. However, I've found that most families can reach satisfactory resolutions by maintaining open communication, showing empathy for different perspectives, and remaining focused on preserving relationships above possessions.

Ultimately, the most successful resolutions to conflicts over shared and inherited items come when families approach the process with patience, creativity, and a commitment to maintaining strong relationships. By focusing on honoring memories and preserving family bonds rather than claiming possessions, families can transform potential sources of conflict into opportunities for deeper connection and understanding.

Supporting Elderly Parents Through the Transition

Supporting elderly parents through the downsizing process requires a delicate balance of compassion, patience, and practical guidance. Through my experience helping three elderly couples transition to smaller homes, I've learned that success lies not in forcing change, but in fostering collaboration and understanding throughout the journey.

One of the most important lessons came while helping the Hendersons prepare for their move to a retirement community. Mrs. Henderson initially resisted every suggestion, but when we shifted our approach to focus on her vision for this next chapter of life, everything changed. Instead of telling her what she needed to do, we started by asking her to share her hopes and concerns for the future.

When approaching downsizing conversations with elderly parents, several key principles help create a supportive environment:

- Begin by listening to their hopes and concerns
- Focus on the positive aspects of the transition
- Take time to understand their emotional attachments
- Break the process into small, manageable steps
- Celebrate progress and respect their pace

One particularly effective approach I've developed is what I call the 'Life Story Method.' This involves working with parents to document the stories behind their most treasured possessions before making any decisions about what to keep or let go. This process naturally leads to more clarity about which items truly matter most to them.

Working with elderly parents requires understanding that their possessions often represent more than just physical items - they're tangible connections to their life experiences, achievements, and memories. Taking time to honor these connections while helping them envision a more manageable living space can transform resistance into cooperation.

I remember helping Margaret, a retired teacher, prepare for her move to a smaller apartment. Initially overwhelmed by the prospect of sorting through fifty years of teaching materials, we created a 'Legacy Box' where she could preserve her most meaningful teaching moments while letting go of the bulk of her materials. This approach helped her feel that her life's work was being honored rather than discarded.

Practical strategies that support successful transitions include:

- Create a system for documenting important memories
- Photograph items before letting them go
- Consider creating memory books or digital archives
- Help identify items that will fit well in the new space
- Maintain familiar arrangements where possible

It's crucial to involve other family members in the process while maintaining clear communication and shared responsibilities. Creating a support network ensures that no single person bears the entire emotional and physical burden of the transition. Regular family meetings can help keep everyone aligned and provide opportunities to address concerns as they arise.

When working with elderly parents, timing and pacing are everything. I've found that shorter, more frequent sessions often work better than marathon sorting days. This approach helps prevent physical and emotional exhaustion while allowing time for processing decisions between sessions.

Remember that this transition often represents a significant life change for elderly parents, and their emotions may fluctuate throughout the process. Patience and empathy are essential, as is maintaining a balance between progress and sensitivity to their needs.

One of the most effective tools I've used is creating a floor plan of the new space and using it as a practical guide for decision-making. This visual aid helps parents envision their new home and makes it easier to make practical decisions about what will fit and what needs to find a new home.

Engaging support from family members, friends, or community resources can play a valuable role in this transition. Whether it's help with organizing, moving assistance, or simply providing emotional support, creating a strong support system helps ensure the process moves forward while respecting everyone's physical and emotional limitations.

The ultimate goal isn't just to help elderly parents downsize their possessions, but to support them in transitioning to a new chapter of life with confidence and peace of mind. When approached with patience, understanding, and proper planning, this process can become an opportunity for deeper connection and shared memories rather than a source of stress and conflict.

Establishing Fair Decision-Making Processes

When multiple family members are involved in downsizing decisions, establishing a fair and transparent process becomes crucial for maintaining harmony and making progress. Through my experience helping friends and families navigate these decisions, I've found that having a clear framework not only reduces conflict but helps everyone feel heard and respected throughout the process.

One of the most effective approaches I've seen is what I call the 'Three-Step Consensus' method. This structured approach begins with individual reflection, moves to small group discussions, and concludes with full family agreement. This layered process allows everyone to fully consider their own priorities before engaging in broader family negotiations.

Key elements for establishing fair decision-making processes include:

- Document all decisions in writing
- Set clear timelines for each decision phase

- Create a system for tracking items under discussion

- Establish a process for handling disagreements

- Maintain transparency throughout the process

While helping the Anderson family downsize their parents' home, we implemented what became known as the 'Priority Pass' system. Each family member received three 'priority passes' they could use to claim items of special significance to them. This simple approach helped prevent conflicts over the most emotionally charged items while ensuring everyone had equal opportunity to secure their most treasured pieces.

The key to successful decision-making often lies in separating emotional value from practical considerations. Creating two distinct evaluation criteria - one for items with significant emotional attachment and another for practical household goods - helps prevent emotional overwhelm while ensuring necessary items are properly distributed.

One particularly effective tool that emerged through my downsizing experiences is the 'Decision Matrix' - a simple grid where family members can rate items based on both practical utility and emotional significance. This visual aid often helps clarify priorities and makes it easier to reach consensus on challenging decisions.

When helping the Fraser family sort through their grandmother's estate, we discovered that taking photographs of contested items and creating a digital catalog allowed everyone to step back and make more objective decisions. This distance often led to more thoughtful choices and creative solutions, such as taking turns hosting family heirlooms or creating memory books instead of keeping all physical items.

Remember that fair doesn't always mean equal. Sometimes the most equitable solution might not be splitting everything evenly, but rather ensuring that each person's core needs and emotional attachments are honored. The goal is to create a process that feels just and respectful to all involved.

Consider these strategies for maintaining fairness throughout the decision-making process:

- Consider rotating possession of shared items
- Create systems for sharing digital memories
- Establish clear guidelines for future decisions
- Build in flexibility for unique situations
- Focus on long-term family harmony

One strategy that has proven particularly effective is implementing 'cooling off' periods for difficult decisions. When emotions run high, taking a structured break allows everyone to reflect and often leads to more collaborative solutions. Setting specific timeframes for these breaks ensures the process continues moving forward.

The most successful decision-making processes I've witnessed are those that remain flexible enough to adapt to family dynamics while maintaining clear structure and fairness. It's about finding the right balance between efficiency and emotional consideration, between individual wishes and group harmony.

While helping one family navigate their downsizing journey, they created what they called their 'Legacy Council' - regular meetings where they not only made decisions about current items but also established guidelines for handling future inherited possessions. This proactive approach helped prevent future conflicts while honoring their family's history and values.

Regular assessment and adjustment of your decision-making process helps ensure continued effectiveness:

- Schedule regular check-ins to assess process effectiveness

- Adjust approaches based on family feedback

- Document successful strategies for future reference

- Celebrate collaborative decisions

- Keep focus on strengthening family bonds

Remember that the goal of establishing fair decision-making processes isn't just about distributing possessions - it's about preserving and strengthening family relationships through respectful collaboration. When families focus on this broader perspective, they often find creative solutions that honor both individual needs and collective harmony.

Managing Different Emotional Attachments to Possessions

Navigating different emotional attachments to shared possessions is one of the most delicate aspects of family downsizing. Through helping several elderly couples and extended families work through their downsizing journeys, I've observed that these varying emotional connections often become a source of misunderstanding when not properly acknowledged and addressed.

I witnessed this firsthand while helping three siblings sort through their childhood home. The eldest approached items primarily through a practical lens, focusing on utility and future need. The middle sibling had deep emotional attachments to childhood memorabilia, while the youngest struggled most with items that represented family traditions and gatherings. Understanding and honoring these different perspectives became crucial to moving forward productively.

One effective approach I've found useful is what I call the 'Emotional Mapping Exercise.' Family members use different colored stickers to indicate their level of attachment to various items before any decisions are made. This visual representation often helps family members understand and respect each other's emotional connections while making it easier to identify items that hold special significance for multiple people.

It's crucial to understand that emotional attachments to possessions often run deeper than the items themselves. They can represent connections to loved ones, reminders of important life events, or symbols of personal achievements. Acknowledging these deeper meanings helps create a more compassionate and effective downsizing process.

While helping a friend sort through her mother's kitchen items, we discovered that what appeared to be an ordinary kitchen timer held deep significance - it was the last gift her grandmother had given her before passing. Understanding these hidden emotional connections helps prevent unintentional hurt and allows for more sensitive decision-making.

Several strategies can help families navigate different emotional attachments:

- Take time to share stories about meaningful items

- Look for creative ways to preserve memories without keeping everything

- Consider creating memory books or digital archives

- Focus on the essence of what makes items meaningful

- Find ways to honor emotions while making practical decisions

A particularly effective strategy that emerged through my experiences is implementing what I call 'Emotional Processing Periods.' These are designated times when family members can share stories and memories associated with items before any decisions about their fate are made. This approach often naturally leads to more collaborative and understanding decisions about what to keep, share, or let go.

It's also important to recognize that emotional attachments can shift throughout the downsizing process. What seems impossible to part with at the beginning might feel less essential after proper acknowledgment and processing. Allowing time for these emotional shifts can make the entire process more manageable and successful.

One tool that has proven particularly helpful is the 'Memory Preservation Box.' Each family member receives a designated space to keep their most emotionally significant items, with the understanding that everything must fit within that space. This physical boundary helps guide difficult decisions while ensuring everyone's most treasured possessions are preserved.

While helping a middle-aged friend downsize her home, we created what she called her 'Legacy Library' - a beautiful combination of physical items, photographs, and written stories that captured the essence of her most emotionally charged possessions without keeping everything. This approach allowed her to honor her attachments while creating space for new experiences.

Remember that managing different emotional attachments isn't about determining whose feelings are 'right' or 'wrong' - it's about creating a process that honors and respects each person's emotional connection while moving forward with necessary changes. Success comes from finding ways to preserve what matters most while letting go of the physical items that no longer serve our present needs.

Through my own downsizing experiences and helping others, I've learned that acknowledging and working with different emotional attachments, rather than trying to override them, leads to more successful and harmonious outcomes. When family members feel their emotional connections are understood and respected, they're often more willing to engage in the practical aspects of downsizing with an open mind.

Creating Healthy Boundaries During the Downsizing Process

Setting and maintaining healthy boundaries during downsizing is crucial, especially when working with family members or managing well-meaning friends who want to be involved. Through my experience helping several families navigate this process, I've discovered that clear boundaries not only protect relationships but also ensure the process moves forward effectively.

When helping a recently widowed friend downsize her family home, I witnessed firsthand how well-meaning relatives offering unsolicited advice and attempting to take control could overwhelm the process. Together, we developed what we called her 'Downsizing Declaration' - a clear statement of her preferences, timeline, and decision-making process that she could share with family members.

> Several key elements help establish effective boundaries during downsizing:
> - Establish clear roles and responsibilities
> - Set specific times for family involvement
> - Create guidelines for decision-making authority
> - Communicate boundaries respectfully but firmly
> - Define consequences for boundary violations

Boundaries aren't just about limiting others' involvement - they're about protecting your own emotional and physical energy during the downsizing process. Consider creating what I call 'Sacred Space Hours' - designated times when you can work on downsizing without interruption or influence from others.

Another crucial aspect of boundary-setting involves managing the flow of new items into your space during the downsizing process. While helping the Anderson family downsize, we implemented a 'Pause Period' - agreeing that no new items would be acquired during their three-month downsizing project unless absolutely necessary. This boundary helped prevent the common problem of items creeping back in while trying to clear space.

It's also important to establish boundaries around the pace of the process. Rushing through downsizing decisions often leads to regret or poor choices. Creating a realistic timeline that includes buffer zones for emotional processing and rest has proven invaluable in my experience helping friends and family downsize.

One particularly effective boundary-setting tool I've found useful is the 'Three-Question Filter' for managing others' involvement:1. Is this person's input necessary for this decision?2. Will their involvement help or hinder the process?3. How will their participation affect my emotional well-being?

These questions help maintain appropriate boundaries while still benefiting from genuine help when needed.

Remember that boundaries aren't walls - they're guidelines that help protect your energy and ensure the downsizing process serves your needs. Good boundaries actually strengthen relationships by preventing resentment and maintaining clear expectations.

I recall helping a friend who struggled with family members dropping off items they thought he 'might want' during his downsizing process. We created a simple but effective boundary statement: 'I appreciate your thoughtfulness, but I'm not accepting any new items during this transition. I'd be happy to share my progress with you during our weekly family dinner.' This clear, kind response helped him maintain control of his space while preserving family relationships.

Several strategies can help maintain healthy boundaries:

- Create clear communication templates for common situations

- Practice expressing boundaries confidently but kindly

- Document agreements and expectations

- Review and adjust boundaries as needed

- Celebrate successful boundary maintenance

It's also crucial to establish boundaries around the decision-making process itself. While input from others can be valuable, ultimate authority over your possessions should remain with you. I encourage creating a 'Decision Zone' - identifying which choices you'll make independently and which might benefit from family input.

Finally, remember that maintaining boundaries requires ongoing attention and occasional reinforcement. Like any new skill, it becomes easier with practice and consistent application. The goal isn't to isolate yourself but to create a supportive environment that honors your downsizing journey while maintaining healthy relationships with those around you.

Over time I've learned that clear, consistent boundaries create the foundation for successful transitions. When everyone understands and respects these guidelines, the process becomes more manageable and relationships often grow stronger through the experience.As we conclude this chapter on family dynamics and downsizing, it's important to recognize that the path to successful family downsizing lies in understanding, respecting, and working with the complex web of relationships and emotions involved. Throughout my experiences helping friends and family members through their downsizing journeys, I've witnessed how approaching these transitions with patience, empathy, and clear communication can transform what might be a challenging process into an opportunity for deeper family connection.

The Thompson family's story, which we explored earlier in this chapter, perfectly illustrates how implementing structured approaches like the 'Sunday Circle' can help navigate complex family dynamics. Their journey from tension to collaboration demonstrates that with the right tools and mindset, families can work together effectively while preserving and even strengthening their relationships.

Remember that every family's downsizing journey is unique, shaped by their individual dynamics, histories, and emotional attachments to possessions. The strategies we've discussed - from establishing clear communication protocols to managing different emotional attachments and setting healthy boundaries - are meant to be adapted to your family's specific needs and circumstances.

Through my work with elderly couples and friends navigating their own downsizing journeys, I've seen that the most successful family transitions share a few common threads: mutual respect, clear communication, fair decision-making, and healthy boundaries. When these elements are in place, families are better equipped to move through the challenges of downsizing while preserving what matters most—their relationships with one another.

As you step into your own family downsizing process, keep in mind that the goal isn't only to clear out physical space—it's to create an environment where everyone feels heard, supported, and valued. Make time to celebrate the small milestones, acknowledge the emotional moments, and appreciate the deeper connections that often emerge along the way.

The skills you build during this process—learning to communicate with care, set thoughtful boundaries, and navigate emotional terrain—are more than just tools for downsizing. They're tools for life. These moments of growth will continue to support you through future transitions and strengthen the bonds you share with those closest to you.

As we close this chapter, I encourage you to bring patience, compassion, and a steady heart to the journey ahead. The true success of a family downsizing project isn't just measured in cleared shelves or empty rooms—it's measured in the strength, trust, and understanding you carry forward together.

Chapter Five

The Life Simplification Method

Organizing What Remains

After the thoughtful work of deciding what to keep, the next important step is creating systems that help your carefully chosen belongings support your life with ease and purpose. Just like a well-tended garden, where each plant has its own space to grow and thrive, the items you've chosen to keep deserve thoughtful placement—so they continue to serve you, not overwhelm you.

This phase is where your downsizing efforts begin to take root. Organizing what remains isn't just about assigning spots on a shelf—it's about creating harmony between your space and the way you live. When your surroundings reflect your daily routines, everything flows more smoothly. Think of it like choreographing a quiet, purposeful dance—each item finding its natural place in the rhythm of your home.

The real challenge isn't simply where to put things—it's creating systems that work *with* your habits, not against them. Too often, people try to fit themselves into rigid organizing methods that don't match how they naturally move through their day. The result? Frustration, clutter creep, and systems that quietly fall apart over time. The key is designing a space that feels intuitive—one that supports your routines, adapts to your needs, and makes daily life feel a little lighter.

I saw this principle come to life while working with my friend Lisa, a freelance graphic designer who had done the hard work of downsizing but found herself frustrated by the ongoing challenge of staying organized—especially in her home office. Like many creative people, Lisa's workflow thrived on flexibility. Traditional organizing systems felt too rigid and stifling, more like a constraint than a solution.

Together, we created what we called the "Creative Flow System"—an organizing approach that matched her style instead of forcing her to conform to someone else's. We set up modular storage zones that could shift easily depending on her current projects, designed a color-coded digital filing system that mirrored her physical workspace, and added a simple five-minute end-of-day reset routine to help her stay grounded without feeling overwhelmed.

The real breakthrough came when we realized that organization doesn't have to be rigid to be effective—it can be just as fluid and adaptable as the person using it. Within a few weeks, Lisa wasn't just maintaining her space—she was thriving in it. She told me she felt more focused, more creative, and more at ease simply because she could find what she needed without the mental clutter of searching through chaos.

Her story is a reminder that the right organizing system doesn't require perfection—it just needs to support your natural habits and help your space work *with* you, not against you.

In this chapter, we'll explore how to create organizational systems that feel as natural as breathing. You'll learn how to identify your personal patterns and preferences, design storage solutions that support rather than restrict your lifestyle, and implement routines that maintain order without feeling overwhelming. Whether you're organizing a small apartment or a spacious home, the principles we'll discuss can be adapted to any living situation, ensuring that your simplified space continues to support and inspire your daily life.

Creating Functional Zones in Your Living Spaces

One of the most powerful ways to maintain organization after downsizing is to establish clear functional zones within your living spaces. Think of your home as a well-designed workplace where each area serves a specific purpose. By designating distinct areas for different activities, you create natural boundaries that help prevent clutter and maintain order.

When helping my elderly neighbor downsize her home, I noticed she was struggling because everything was happening everywhere - paying bills at the kitchen counter, doing craft projects on her bed, and storing office supplies in the living room. Together, we reimagined her space by creating dedicated zones for specific activities, and the transformation was remarkable.

Start by considering these essential zones that most homes need:

- **Entry Zone:** A designated space for shoes, keys, and incoming items

- **Rest Zone**: Bedrooms and quiet areas for relaxation

- **Work Zone**: A dedicated space for productive tasks

- **Social Zone**: Areas for entertaining and family gathering

- **Storage Zone:** Organized spaces for less-frequently used items

The key to successful zoning lies in understanding your daily routines and natural patterns. Start by observing how you actually use your space rather than how you think you should use it. Track your movements and activities for a few days to identify your natural patterns and preferences. This information will help you create zones that support rather than fight against your habits.

When establishing zones, consider the principle of frequency and access. Items used daily should be stored in easily accessible locations within their respective zones. For instance, in your kitchen zone, everyday dishes should be within easy reach, while special occasion serving pieces can be stored in less accessible areas. This principle applies to every zone in your home.

One particularly effective approach is creating what I call 'micro-zones' within larger spaces. For example, in my living room, I created a reading nook with good lighting, a comfortable chair, and a small shelf for current books, establishing a dedicated space within the larger room. These micro-zones help maintain order by giving specific activities their own home within a multi-purpose space.

The beauty of functional zones lies in their ability to grow and adapt with your needs. In my own home, I discovered that some zones needed adjustment as my routines changed. Don't be afraid to experiment and modify your zones until they feel natural and supportive of your lifestyle. Remember that zones don't have to be rigid or permanent - they can be as simple as a designated corner for meditation or as complex as a multi-purpose craft area that transforms into a guest space when needed.

One common challenge in creating functional zones is dealing with overlap in small spaces. If you're working with limited square footage, consider using mobile solutions or dual-purpose furniture that can help define different zones without requiring permanent divisions. Folding screens, rolling carts, or furniture that can be easily rearranged can help create temporary boundaries when needed.

The most successful zoning systems feel almost invisible to the people using them. When zones are properly established, they guide your movements and activities naturally, making it easier to maintain order without conscious effort. Think of it as creating a gentle current that guides you through your space, rather than building rigid walls that restrict movement.

Remember to keep your zones focused but flexible. Life changes, and your spaces should be able to adapt along with it. The goal isn't to create a rigid system of rules but rather to develop an intuitive flow that makes your daily activities more effortless and enjoyable.

Implementing the One-Touch Rule for Daily Organization

Among the most transformative principles for maintaining an organized space is the One-Touch Rule - a beautifully simple concept that revolutionizes how we handle our possessions. The core idea is elegantly straightforward: handle items only once when dealing with them. Instead of moving papers from one pile to another or relocating items from surface to surface, make an immediate decision about where they belong and take action accordingly.

I discovered the power of this rule in my own home when I noticed I had developed a habit of creating multiple 'staging areas' for items - moving things from my desk to a side table, then to a box, and finally to their permanent home, if they made it there at all. By implementing the One-Touch Rule, I eliminated these intermediate steps and the clutter they created.

The beauty of this rule lies in its versatility across different areas of daily life:

- **Mail:** Sort immediately into action, file, or recycle

- **Laundry:** Put clothes away directly from the dryer

- **Shopping:** Unpack and store items in their designated spots immediately

- **Digital files:** Save documents directly to their proper folders

- **Daily items**: Return things to their homes immediately after use

The simplicity of this rule masks its profound impact on both our physical spaces and mental energy. Every time we handle an item without making a final decision about it, we create what I think of as 'decision debt' - the mental burden of knowing we'll need to deal with it again later. By making immediate decisions and taking action, we free up mental space and reduce the cognitive load of maintaining our organized spaces.

One common challenge I've noticed when implementing this rule is the tendency to delay decisions when we're unsure about where something belongs. To address this, I learned to create a simple decision tree for common items. For instance, when handling incoming mail, your options might be: act on it immediately, file it, or recycle it. Having these clear categories eliminates the temptation to create a 'deal with it later' pile.

The One-Touch Rule becomes particularly powerful when combined with designated zones in your home. When every item has a clear 'home,' making immediate decisions about where things belong becomes much easier. I experienced this firsthand when organizing my garage workshop. By establishing specific zones for different types of tools and implementing the One-Touch Rule, I transformed my workspace from a cluttered maze into an efficient, well-organized area.

Implementation requires both physical and mental preparation. First, ensure that storage solutions are easily accessible - if putting something away requires moving three other items first, you're less likely to follow through. Second, practice mindful awareness when handling items. Before moving something, pause and ask yourself: 'Where does this belong, and can I put it there now?'

It's important to note that the One-Touch Rule isn't about perfection - it's about progress. There will be times when following this rule strictly isn't practical, and that's okay. The goal is to make it your default approach while allowing for flexibility when needed. For instance, during particularly busy mornings or when dealing with unexpected situations, you might need to temporarily set items aside. The key is returning to the principle as your standard practice.

To build this habit effectively, start small. Choose one area or category of items to practice with, such as mail or dishes, and gradually expand as the behavior becomes more natural. Remember that like any new habit, implementing the One-Touch Rule requires patience and consistency. The effort invested in developing this practice pays dividends in time saved and reduced stress from managing your possessions.

The One-Touch Rule also serves as a powerful filter for future acquisitions. When considering new purchases, thinking about where items will live and how they'll fit into your one-touch system can help prevent unnecessary accumulation. This forward-thinking approach supports your long-term goals for maintaining a simplified, organized living space.

Through my journey of helping others embrace simpler living, I've seen how the One-Touch Rule can transform even the most cluttered spaces into efficient, peaceful environments. It's not just about keeping things tidy - it's about creating a sustainable system that supports your daily life and preserves the mental energy often wasted on repeated decision-making.

Designing Custom Storage Solutions for Different Item Categories

Creating effective storage solutions is like designing a custom-built home for your possessions - each category of items requires thoughtful consideration of its unique needs and usage patterns. Through my own downsizing journey and experiences helping friends and family maintain their simplified spaces, I've discovered that the most successful storage solutions are those that align perfectly with how items are actually used in daily life.

Last summer, while helping my elderly neighbor Rachel reorganize her kitchen, we had an enlightening experience that transformed how I approach storage design. Instead of using standard drawer dividers and cabinet organizers, we carefully analyzed her cooking habits and created zones based on her workflow. We installed pull-out shelves for heavy pots, vertical dividers for baking sheets, and a custom spice organization system within arm's reach of her primary cooking area. The result wasn't just organized storage - it was a kitchen that actively supported her love of cooking.

Essential Storage Principles:

- Design for frequency of use

- Consider item weight and size

- Plan for easy maintenance

- Allow room for growth

- Prioritize visibility and accessibility

- Incorporate modular solutions

The key to successful storage design lies in understanding the unique characteristics of different item categories. Books require different solutions than clothing, which in turn need different approaches than kitchen items or hobby supplies. Start by analyzing the specific needs of each category: How often are these items used? Do they need protection from light or moisture? Are they seasonal? Do they need to be visible or hidden?

In my own home, I've implemented what I call the 'category-specific approach' to storage. For example, my sewing supplies are stored in clear, stackable containers with detailed labels, making it easy to see what I have while protecting materials from dust. Meanwhile, my seasonal clothing is stored in vacuum-sealed bags with cedar blocks, addressing both space efficiency and preservation needs.

Category-Specific Storage Solutions:

- **Clothing:** Breathable containers with humidity control

- **Documents:** Fire-safe boxes for important papers

- **Electronics:** Dust-free, ventilated storage

- **Seasonal items:** Protective, space-saving solutions

- **Hobby supplies:** Visible, accessible organization

One particularly effective strategy is the 'modular matrix' approach. This system uses interchangeable storage components that can be reconfigured as needs change. When helping my friend Maria transition from a house to an apartment, I suggested this system throughout her space. The modular components allowed her to adjust her storage solutions as she settled into her new lifestyle, without needing to purchase new organizational tools.

Remember that the best storage solutions often combine multiple approaches. For instance, in a home office, you might use a combination of visible storage for frequently accessed supplies, closed storage for visual clarity, and archival storage for important documents. The goal is to create a system that feels intuitive and supports your natural habits.

Don't be afraid to think creatively when designing storage solutions. The most effective systems I've seen have often been unconventional. My sister transformed an old armoire into a gift-wrapping station with rotating dowels for ribbon storage and custom-sized shelves for paper. The key was focusing on how she actually used these items rather than following traditional storage conventions.

Maintenance is another crucial factor to consider when designing storage solutions. The most beautiful and efficient system will fail if it's too complicated to maintain. I always follow what I call the '30-second rule' - if it takes longer than 30 seconds to put something away, you're less likely to do it consistently. This principle has guided countless storage solutions in my home, ensuring they remain functional long after the initial organization.

Finally, remember that storage solutions should evolve with your needs. Build in flexibility whenever possible, and plan for periodic reviews and adjustments. This adaptability ensures your storage systems continue to serve you effectively as your lifestyle changes and evolves.

Establishing Daily Reset Routines

Creating daily reset routines is like establishing a gentle rhythm that keeps your simplified space in harmony. These routines serve as anchors throughout your day, preventing the slow creep of clutter and maintaining the serenity you've worked so hard to achieve. When incorporated mindfully into your daily life, reset routines become natural transition points that help you maintain order without feeling overwhelmed.

Through my own journey of maintaining a simplified home, I've discovered that the most effective reset routines align with our natural daily patterns. For instance, my morning reset routine has become as automatic as brewing my first cup of coffee - a quick sweep through the bathroom, making the bed, and ensuring surfaces are clear before starting my day.

Essential Daily Reset Components:

- **Morning Reset:** Quick bed-making and bathroom tidying

- **Midday Reset**: Surface clearing and quick item returns

- **Evening Reset**: 15-minute whole-home reset before bed

- **Weekly Reset:** Deeper check of systems and spaces

The key to successful reset routines lies in their simplicity and integration into your natural daily patterns. Rather than viewing them as additional tasks to complete, think of them as transitional moments that help you shift between different parts of your day. Your evening reset routine can serve as a calming ritual that signals to your body and mind that it's time to wind down.

I experienced the transformative power of reset routines firsthand when helping my elderly neighbor maintain her newly organized space. Together, we created what we called her 'Sunset Sweep' - a simple evening routine that included returning items to their homes, clearing countertops, and preparing for the next day. Within weeks, she shared how these small actions had not only maintained her space but also improved her sleep quality by reducing evening anxiety.

One particularly effective strategy I've found is the '2-Minute Rule' for reset routines: if you notice something that needs attention and it will take less than two minutes to address, do it immediately. This prevents the accumulation of small tasks that can feel overwhelming when tackled all at once.

Reset Routine Building Blocks:

- Clear horizontal surfaces

- Return items to their homes

- Process incoming items immediately

- Quick sweep of high-traffic areas

- Reset furniture to original positions

The beauty of reset routines lies in their cumulative impact. While each individual action might seem small, together they create a powerful system for maintaining order. I witnessed this in my own home when I first implemented these routines. What once felt like a constant battle against chaos transformed into a gentle flow of maintenance that required minimal effort.

One common challenge I see is the tendency to create overly ambitious reset routines that become unsustainable. Start small and build gradually. For instance, begin with a simple evening routine of clearing the kitchen counters and preparing for the next morning. As this becomes habitual, you can add additional elements that support your lifestyle.

Remember that reset routines should be flexible enough to adapt to different circumstances while maintaining their core purpose. During particularly busy periods, you might need to scale back to just the essentials. The goal is progress, not perfection.

To help establish these routines, create what I call 'Reset Anchors' - specific triggers that remind you to perform your reset activities. These might be finishing dinner (evening kitchen reset), brushing your teeth (bathroom reset), or hearing a certain notification on your phone (midday reset). By linking these routines to existing habits, they become more natural and easier to maintain.

My friend Sarah found success by turning her reset routines into a family activity. Every evening after dinner, her family spends 10 minutes doing what they call the 'Sunset Sweep' - each person responsible for resetting a different zone of their home. This not only maintains their space but also teaches her children valuable organizational habits.

The most successful reset routines feel less like chores and more like acts of self-care. They're opportunities to create order in your external environment, which often leads to greater mental clarity and reduced stress. Think of these routines as gifts to your future self - small actions today that make tomorrow run more smoothly.

Maintaining Flexibility in Organizational Systems

Creating flexible organizational systems is essential for long-term success in maintaining an organized space. Like a well-designed city that evolves with its inhabitants, your organizational systems should be able to adapt and grow with your changing needs. Through years of maintaining my own simplified space and helping others with theirs, I've learned that rigid systems often break down when life inevitably throws us curveballs.

When helping my friend Emma adapt her home office during her transition to remote work, we discovered the importance of what I call the 'Flex-Zone Principle.' Rather than creating fixed storage solutions, we designed areas that could easily transform based on her current projects while maintaining overall organization. This adaptable approach proved invaluable as her work evolved and her needs changed throughout the year.

The key to maintaining flexibility lies in creating systems with built-in adaptability. Think of your organizational solutions like a well-designed wardrobe that can transition seamlessly between seasons - core pieces remain constant while others rotate based on current needs. This approach ensures your systems can grow and contract with your needs while maintaining fundamental organization.

One particularly effective strategy is the '80/20 Space Rule' - designing storage systems to be about 80% full, leaving 20% for growth and change. This buffer zone prevents systems from becoming overcrowded and allows for natural fluctuations in your possessions without requiring a complete reorganization. For instance, I maintain this rule in my kitchen cabinets, which allows me to easily accommodate new items or temporarily store extra supplies without disrupting the existing organization.

When helping my elderly neighbor transition to a smaller space, we implemented what I call 'Stage-Ready Storage' - organizational systems that could easily evolve as her needs changed. Instead of creating fixed storage solutions, we designed flexible systems using modular components that could be reconfigured as needed. This approach has allowed her to maintain an organized space despite significant changes in her lifestyle and needs.

The concept of flexible organization extends beyond physical spaces to digital realms as well. In my own experience organizing digital files, I've found that creating broad category folders with adjustable sub-categories works better than highly specific organizational structures that become difficult to navigate as needs change.

Perhaps most importantly, maintaining flexible systems requires regular evaluation and adjustment. I recommend scheduling quarterly 'Flexibility Checks' - brief reviews of your organizational systems to ensure they're still serving your current needs. These reviews help identify areas that need adjustment before they become problematic.

Through my own downsizing journey, I've found that the most successful long-term organization comes from systems that feel natural and intuitive while remaining adaptable to change. It's about finding the sweet spot between structure and flexibility, creating systems that support your life rather than constrain it.

When helping my friend Lisa organize her growing children's playroom, we created what we called 'Growth Zones' - areas that could easily transition from baby toys to preschool activities to school projects. The key was using adjustable shelving systems and clear, broad categories that could evolve with the children's changing interests and needs.

One common challenge I've observed is the tendency to over-categorize, creating such specific organizational systems that they become difficult to maintain as needs change. Instead, focus on broader categories with adjustable sub-categories. This approach provides structure while maintaining adaptability. For example, rather than creating separate categories for every type of crafting supply, group items by general purpose with the flexibility to refine the organization as needed.

Remember that flexibility in organization doesn't mean constantly changing everything - it means having the ability to make adjustments when needed while maintaining the core principles that keep your space functional and peaceful. Think of it as creating a living system that grows and evolves with you, rather than a static set of rules that might eventually break under pressure.

Regular maintenance of flexible systems involves not just physical organization but also mindset flexibility. Be open to questioning and adjusting your systems when they no longer serve their purpose effectively. Sometimes the most organized solution is one that breaks traditional organizational rules but works perfectly for your specific needs and lifestyle.

Digital Organization Strategies for Modern Living

In our increasingly digital world, organizing our virtual spaces has become just as crucial as maintaining our physical environments. Digital clutter can be just as overwhelming as physical clutter, often more insidious because it's less visible but equally capable of creating stress and reducing productivity. Through my experience helping family and friends navigate digital organization, I've discovered that the same principles that guide physical decluttering can be effectively applied to our digital lives.

One of my most enlightening experiences came while helping my friend Jennifer, a freelance writer struggling with digital chaos. Her computer desktop was cluttered with hundreds of files, her email inbox contained thousands of unread messages, and she had countless duplicate photos across multiple devices. Together, we developed what we called the 'Digital Sanctuary System' - a comprehensive approach to creating and maintaining order in her digital world.

The foundation of effective digital organization lies in creating intuitive folder structures that mirror how you think and work. Just as we create zones in physical spaces, digital spaces need clear, logical organization that supports your natural workflow. Start by establishing main categories for your files, then create subcategories that make sense for your specific needs.

Digital Organization Focus Areas:

- File management and folder structure

- Email organization and inbox maintenance

- Photo storage and backup systems

- Password management and digital security

- Cloud storage optimization

- App and software organization

A particularly effective strategy that emerged from my own digital organization journey is the 'Digital Home Base' concept - designating one primary location for each type of digital asset. For instance, choosing one cloud service for photo storage, another for document backup, and a specific location for project files. This eliminates the confusion of searching multiple locations for files and reduces the likelihood of creating duplicate copies.

Email management often presents one of the biggest digital organization challenges. Through trial and error in my own life, I've developed what I call the '2-2-2 System': spending two minutes twice a day processing emails, with no email sitting in your inbox longer than two days. This approach helps prevent the overwhelming accumulation of unread messages while ensuring important communications don't get lost.

Photo organization deserves special attention in our digital age. I recommend creating a systematic approach to photo management that includes regular importing, immediate deletion of poor-quality images, and consistent naming conventions. My personal photo management system uses what I call the 'Photo Priority System' - organizing photos into three main categories: must-keep memories, useful reference images, and temporary photos that can be deleted after serving their purpose.

Digital security should be an integral part of your organization strategy. When helping my elderly neighbor set up her digital systems, we implemented a password management system to maintain secure, unique passwords while keeping them organized and accessible. Regular backups of important files should be automated, with at least one cloud-based backup and one physical backup for crucial documents.

One often overlooked aspect of digital organization is app management. Just as we declutter physical spaces, regularly review and remove unused apps from your devices. In my own phone and tablet organization, I create what I call 'App Zones' - grouping applications by function or frequency of use to make them easier to locate and access.

Remember that digital organization, like physical organization, requires regular maintenance. Schedule monthly 'Digital Declutter Sessions' to review and clean up your digital spaces. These sessions might include clearing out old downloads, archiving completed project files, or consolidating scattered documents into their proper locations.

Perhaps most importantly, establish boundaries with your digital life. Just as we create limits for physical possessions, set guidelines for digital accumulation. This might mean unsubscribing from unnecessary email lists, limiting app downloads, or regularly reviewing and deleting unused digital content.

The goal of digital organization isn't perfection - it's creating systems that support your productivity and peace of mind while reducing digital stress and overwhelm. Think of your digital spaces as extensions of your physical spaces, deserving the same level of intentional organization and maintenance. As we conclude this chapter on organizing what remains after downsizing, remember that the goal isn't creating perfect systems, but rather developing intuitive organizational methods that support and enhance your daily life. Through examples like Lisa's Creative Flow System, we've seen how personalized organizational approaches can transform spaces from sources of stress into foundations for productivity and peace.

The journey of organizing your simplified space is deeply personal, requiring solutions as unique as your lifestyle. Whether it's creating functional zones that support your natural patterns, implementing the One-Touch Rule to prevent clutter accumulation, or developing flexible systems that grow with your needs, each strategy we've discussed can be adapted to fit your specific circumstances. The digital organization strategies we've explored recognize that modern living requires attention to both physical and virtual spaces, creating harmony across all aspects of our lives.

Perhaps most importantly, we've learned that successful organization isn't about forcing yourself into rigid systems or following someone else's rules. It's about understanding your natural habits and creating supportive structures that enhance rather than restrict your lifestyle. As you move forward with implementing these strategies in your own space, remember to be patient with yourself. Start with small changes, celebrate your progress, and adjust your systems as needed.

As you continue on your organizational journey, remember that the systems you create should feel like a natural extension of your life—not a rigid structure you have to force yourself into. Whether you're working with a cozy apartment or a larger home, the principles we've explored can be adapted to fit your needs, your habits, and your preferences. The goal is to find that sweet spot—a balance of structure and flexibility that keeps your space working for you, not against you.

In the next chapter, we'll build on this foundation by exploring how to sustain these systems over time through simple habits and daily routines. Because while setting up your space is an important step, keeping it flowing smoothly is what truly makes lasting change possible. The systems you put in place today are more than just organizing tools—they're the groundwork for a home that continues to support and inspire your everyday life.

And just know—your future self will thank you for the effort you're putting in now. Organization isn't about striving for perfection. It's about creating a space that helps you feel calm, clear, and supported. As you apply these ideas, focus on steady progress, not flawless execution. Let your systems evolve with you, and trust that the real joy comes not just from how a space looks—but from how it feels to live in it.

Chapter Six

Sustaining Your Clutter-Free Transformation

Building Lasting Habits

Downsizing and simplifying your space is something to be proud of—it's no small accomplishment. But the real magic happens in what comes next: maintaining that sense of freedom day after day, season after season. Like tending a garden, keeping your home clutter-free requires gentle, ongoing care. It's about creating habits that support your vision of a more intentional, peaceful life—not with perfection, but with steady, mindful attention.

Sustaining your progress isn't about willpower—it's about building routines and systems that feel natural and nourishing. When we understand not just the practical steps, but also the emotional and psychological patterns that shape our daily choices, maintenance becomes less of a chore and more of a way to care for ourselves and our space.

Through my work with friends, family, and clients, I've seen a clear pattern: those who maintain their simplified homes over time don't just stick to a checklist—they build a new relationship with their surroundings. They begin to see maintenance not as something to dread, but as a form of self-care. It becomes part of how they stay grounded, organized, and aligned with the life they want to live.

Last year, my friend Rachel—a professional who had recently downsized her apartment—reached out feeling discouraged. Just three months after her initial effort, she was frustrated to see clutter slowly creeping back in. She'd done the hard work of simplifying, but something wasn't sticking. As we talked it through, it became clear: while Rachel had mastered the process of letting go, she hadn't yet built the daily habits needed to maintain her newly organized space.

Together, we came up with a simple but powerful solution we called her "Sunset Reset"—a 15-minute evening routine that included clearing off surfaces, sorting the day's mail, and setting herself up for a calm start the next morning. We also added a monthly "Mindful Review," a gentle check-in where she could reflect on anything new she'd brought into her home and tweak her systems if needed.

The turning point came when Rachel began to treat these routines not as chores, but as small acts of self-care—right alongside her evening skincare ritual or winding down with a good book. Six months later, she told me that not only had her space stayed clutter-free, but her whole mindset around possessions had shifted. Those few minutes of intentional care each day had created lasting change—not through perfection, but through consistency.

Her story is a reminder that sustainable organization isn't about big bursts of energy—it's about small, meaningful actions that align with your values and gently support your everyday life.

In this chapter, we'll explore the essential components of maintaining a clutter-free life: the daily rituals that prevent accumulation, the mindset shifts that support long-term success, and the strategies for adapting your systems as life evolves. We'll delve into practical techniques for building supportive habits while addressing the common challenges that can derail even the most determined downsizers.

Remember, the goal isn't perfection – it's progress. Creating a sustainable, clutter-free life is about developing a flexible framework that can weather life's changes while supporting your vision of simplified living. Through understanding and implementing the principles we'll discuss, you'll be equipped to maintain your downsizing success not just for months, but for years to come.

Creating Daily Maintenance Rituals and Routines

The foundation of a sustainably decluttered life lies in establishing daily maintenance rituals that feel natural and supportive rather than burdensome. These rituals serve as anchors throughout your day, preventing the slow creep of clutter while maintaining the serenity of your simplified space. Having witnessed the transformative power of well-designed routines in my own life and while helping friends and family maintain their downsizing success, I've found that the most effective routines are those that align with your natural daily rhythm and energy levels.

Consider the power of what I call 'transition moments' – those brief pauses between activities that offer perfect opportunities for quick maintenance tasks. My friend Emma discovered this principle when she created a morning ritual of spending five minutes clearing her bedroom and bathroom surfaces before heading to the kitchen. By the time she prepared her morning coffee, these small actions had already set a positive tone for her day.

- Create a morning reset routine (5-10 minutes)
- Implement the "one-touch rule" for daily items
- Establish evening cleanup rituals
- Designate specific days for deeper maintenance tasks
- Set up entry/exit routines for managing incoming items

The key to successful maintenance lies not in the complexity of your routines but in their consistency and sustainability. Think of these rituals as small acts of self-care rather than chores. Just as you wouldn't skip brushing your teeth because you're tired, these maintenance routines should become non-negotiable parts of your day.

One particularly effective strategy is the '10-minute sweep' – a focused daily ritual where you move through your main living spaces, returning items to their designated homes and addressing any areas of emerging clutter. This practice helps prevent the accumulation that often leads to overwhelming cleanup sessions later.

Remember that maintenance routines should flex with your life's natural rhythms. During my own journey to simplified living, I noticed that my energy for household tasks peaked in the morning, so I adapted my routines accordingly. Now, I complete my most important maintenance tasks before starting my workday, when my motivation is highest.

One of the most important aspects of maintaining a clutter-free environment is learning to process incoming items effectively. Establish clear protocols for managing mail, packages, and new purchases as they enter your home. Create designated landing zones for items that require action, and make decisions about them promptly rather than allowing them to accumulate.

For families, I often suggest creating 'zone responsibilities' – specific areas that each family member maintains as part of their daily routine. This not only distributes the maintenance workload but also helps instill lasting organizational habits in children while fostering a sense of ownership over shared spaces.

When helping an elderly neighbor downsize her home, I observed how breaking down maintenance tasks into small, manageable portions made them less daunting. Together, we created a simple checklist that aligned with her natural daily patterns, making the upkeep of her newly organized space feel effortless rather than overwhelming.

Remember that perfection isn't the goal – consistency is. Some days, you might only complete a portion of your maintenance routine, and that's perfectly acceptable. The key is to return to your rituals the next day, treating them as supportive practices rather than rigid rules. Over time, these small, consistent actions become the foundation of a sustainably organized and peaceful home.

Developing a Clutter Prevention Mindset

Developing a clutter prevention mindset is like building immunity against the constant flow of possessions that threaten to overwhelm our spaces. Through years of helping friends and family maintain clutter-free homes, I've discovered that maintaining a simplified life isn't just about organizing skills – it's about fundamentally shifting how we think about and interact with our possessions.

One of my most enlightening experiences came while helping Tom, a retired teacher who had successfully downsized but found himself slipping back into old accumulation patterns. When we discussed his challenges, we realized that while he had mastered the physical aspects of organization, his mindset still clung to 'just in case' thinking. Together, we worked to reframe his relationship with possessions, developing what we called his 'intentional acquisition filter' – a mental framework for evaluating potential new items before they entered his home.

- Question the true value and purpose of new acquisitions
- Consider the full cost of ownership (space, maintenance, time)

- Practice the one-in-one-out rule consistently

- Evaluate items based on current lifestyle, not potential future scenarios

- Maintain a wishlist with a waiting period for non-essential purchases

The key to developing a clutter prevention mindset lies in understanding that every item we own demands something from us – space, attention, maintenance, or mental energy. This awareness helps us make more conscious decisions about what we allow into our lives. Those who successfully maintain their clutter-free spaces have internalized this understanding, treating their homes as sacred spaces rather than storage facilities.

One particularly effective strategy I've found helpful is the 'pause and purpose' technique. Before bringing any new item home, pause to consider its specific purpose and place in your life. Will it contribute meaningfully to your daily activities? Does it align with your values and lifestyle goals? This simple practice can dramatically reduce impulsive acquisitions and help maintain the serenity of your simplified space.

Another crucial aspect of clutter prevention is developing what I call 'boundary awareness.' This involves recognizing and respecting the physical and psychological limits of your space. Just as we set boundaries in relationships, we need to establish clear boundaries with our possessions. This might mean limiting certain categories of items to specific spaces or numbers, or regularly assessing whether our belongings still serve their intended purpose.

- Establish clear limits for different categories of items

- Create designated spaces for specific activities and their related items

- Regularly assess the functionality and relevance of possessions

- Practice mindful consumption habits

- Develop strategies for gracefully declining unwanted items

The transformation in mindset often becomes most apparent during gift-giving seasons or sales events. Many of my friends who've embraced simplified living report feeling empowered rather than tempted when faced with opportunities to acquire new things. They've learned to appreciate the freedom that comes with thoughtful consumption over accumulation.

Remember that developing a clutter prevention mindset is a journey, not a destination. It's about progress, not perfection. Each decision to mindfully evaluate new acquisitions strengthens your ability to maintain a simplified life. Through consistent practice, these thought patterns become second nature, creating a natural barrier against the accumulation of unnecessary possessions.

One of the most powerful shifts occurs when you begin to view empty space not as a void to be filled, but as a valuable asset that contributes to your well-being. This perspective helps maintain the breathing room you've created through downsizing, preventing the slow creep of clutter that often occurs when we see empty spaces as opportunities for storage.

By cultivating a clutter prevention mindset, you're not just maintaining an organized space – you're creating a sustainable foundation for the simplified life you envision. This mental framework becomes your first line of defense against the constant pressure to accumulate, allowing you to make conscious choices that align with your values and support your long-term goals for a clutter-free life.

Establishing Boundaries with New Possessions

The art of maintaining a simplified life hinges greatly on how we manage the flow of new items into our homes. Through my journey of helping friends and family maintain their downsizing success, I've discovered that establishing clear boundaries with new possessions isn't just about saying 'no' – it's about creating thoughtful criteria for what deserves a place in our lives.

I recently helped my friend Amanda, a busy mother of two, who had successfully decluttered her home but found herself struggling with the constant influx of new items, especially children's toys and clothing from well-meaning relatives. Together, we developed what we called the 'Sacred Space Protocol' – a set of guidelines that helped her family make mindful decisions about new acquisitions while maintaining harmony with loved ones.

- Create designated holding zones for potential new items

- Implement a 48-hour consideration period for non-essential purchases

- Establish clear criteria for what constitutes a 'need' versus a 'want'

- Set physical space limits for different categories of items

- Develop graceful ways to decline unwanted gifts

The key to successful boundaries lies in their flexibility and practicality. Rather than creating rigid rules that feel restrictive, focus on developing guidelines that support your vision of an intentional life. I've found it helpful to create what I call 'breathing room buffers' – deliberately maintaining some empty space in closets and storage areas to prevent the unconscious tendency to fill every available spot.

One particularly effective strategy is the 'replacement method.' When considering a new item, first identify what it would replace or upgrade in your current collection. This simple practice helps maintain the equilibrium of your simplified space while ensuring that new acquisitions truly add value to your life.

I've observed that successful boundary-setting often requires a shift in how we view our homes. Rather than seeing them as containers that can always accommodate more, we need to treat them as carefully curated spaces where each item earns its place. This mindset helps create natural limits on what we allow through our doors.

Remember that boundaries with possessions often intersect with personal relationships. I emphasize the importance of communicating these boundaries clearly and compassionately with family and friends. One approach that's proven particularly effective is sharing your simplified living goals with loved ones and involving them in your journey rather than simply declaring new rules.

The process of establishing and maintaining boundaries with new possessions becomes easier with practice. Think of it as developing a healthy relationship with your space and belongings. Just as we set boundaries in other areas of our lives to protect our well-being, these material boundaries serve to preserve the serenity and functionality of our simplified spaces.

One of the most powerful aspects of strong boundaries is their ability to reduce decision fatigue. When you have clear criteria for what deserves a place in your home, you spend less mental energy deliberating over potential acquisitions. This clarity creates a natural filter that helps maintain your clutter-free environment without constant conscious effort.

Remember that boundaries aren't about deprivation – they're about protection. They protect the space you've created, the peace you've cultivated, and the simplified lifestyle you've worked hard to achieve. By establishing thoughtful boundaries with new possessions, you're not just maintaining order; you're creating a sustainable foundation for continued freedom from clutter.

Building Support Systems for Long-term Success

Maintaining a simplified life flourishes with the right support system in place. Through my experiences helping friends and family create lasting change through downsizing, I've observed that those who succeed long-term often have strong networks of support that encourage and reinforce their commitment to simplified living.

My friend Jennifer, a marketing professional, had successfully decluttered her home but found herself struggling to maintain her progress in isolation. Together, we created what we called her 'Simplicity Circle' – a small group of like-minded friends who met monthly to share challenges, celebrate victories, and hold each other accountable to their organizational goals.

- Identify potential support partners among friends and family

- Join or create local simplicity circles or minimalist meetups

- Connect with online communities focused on simplified living

- Establish regular check-ins with an accountability partner

- Share your journey with others who might benefit from your experience

The power of community support became evident when Jennifer's group started sharing practical tips and creative solutions for common challenges. One member suggested a seasonal swap meet where they could exchange items they no longer needed, ensuring their possessions found new homes while preventing unnecessary purchases. Another introduced the concept of 'clutter buddies' – partners who help each other maintain their spaces through regular visits and gentle accountability.

Building a support system isn't just about finding people who share your goals – it's about creating an environment that nurtures your commitment to simplified living. This might mean surrounding yourself with individuals who respect your boundaries around possessions or finding mentors who have successfully maintained a clutter-free lifestyle.

One particularly effective strategy I've found is the 'maintenance partnership' model. This involves pairing up with someone who shares similar organizational goals and scheduling regular virtual or in-person sessions to work on maintaining your spaces together. The social connection makes the process more enjoyable while providing built-in accountability.

Remember that support systems can take many forms. For some, it might be a family member who helps maintain shared spaces or a friend who offers encouragement during challenging times. The key is finding what works best for your personality and lifestyle.

I've found that successful support systems often include both practical and emotional components. While having someone to help you maintain physical spaces is valuable, equally important is having individuals who understand and support your vision for a simplified life. These emotional anchors can provide crucial encouragement during times when you might feel tempted to revert to old habits.

Technology can also play a valuable role in building and maintaining support systems. Many people use apps and online platforms to connect with others on similar journeys, share progress photos, and track their maintenance goals. These digital tools can provide additional layers of accountability and inspiration while making it easier to stay connected with your support network.

The beauty of a well-constructed support system is its ability to evolve with your needs. As your lifestyle changes and your simplified living practice deepens, your support network can adapt and grow accordingly. Some individuals who started as novices in their simplicity circles have become mentors themselves, sharing their experiences and inspiring others to embrace a clutter-free life.

Remember that building a support system is an investment in your long-term success. Just as a garden needs regular tending to thrive, your commitment to simplified living benefits from consistent nurturing through supportive relationships and community connections. By intentionally cultivating these support networks, you create a foundation that helps sustain your simplified lifestyle for years to come.

Adapting Habits During Life Transitions

Life transitions, whether planned or unexpected, often present unique challenges to maintaining simplified spaces and organizational habits. Through my experience helping friends and family navigate major life changes, I've discovered that the key to success lies not in rigid adherence to existing systems, but in thoughtful adaptation of habits to meet new circumstances.

One particularly meaningful experience came from helping my friend Lisa, who had maintained an impressively organized home for years until an unexpected job transfer required her to temporarily move in with her sister's family. Initially, Lisa felt her organizational systems crumbling in this shared living situation. Together, we developed what we called 'portable organizing principles' – flexible habits that could adapt to any living situation while maintaining the essence of her simplified lifestyle.

- Create flexible systems that can scale up or down
- Identify core habits that can transfer to any environment
- Develop temporary solutions for transitional periods
- Maintain essential routines while allowing for adaptation
- Build in regular review periods during transitions

The beauty of well-designed organizational habits lies in their adaptability. Rather than viewing transitions as disruptions to our systems, we can see them as opportunities to refine and evolve our approaches to simplified living. This mindset shift helps maintain progress even when circumstances change dramatically.

During major life transitions, it's crucial to identify which habits form the foundation of your organizational success and which ones might need modification. I encourage friends to create what I call a 'habit hierarchy' – prioritizing their organizational practices based on their impact and adaptability to new situations.

For instance, when helping a new retiree adapt to her post-work life, we focused on transforming her work-centered organizational systems to support her new lifestyle. Instead of maintaining her rigid morning office preparation routine, we transformed it into a flexible daily planning session that could accommodate her varying schedule while still providing structure.

- Evaluate which habits are essential versus situational
- Modify routines to match new time patterns and energy levels
- Create transitional systems that bridge old and new habits
- Focus on maintaining core organizational principles
- Document successful adaptations for future transitions

Remember that transitions often require a period of experimentation to find what works in your new situation. During this time, be patient with yourself and view any organizational setbacks as valuable feedback rather than failures. This approach allows you to maintain progress while discovering new ways to support your simplified lifestyle.

One particularly effective strategy I've developed is the 'anchor habit' technique. This involves identifying one or two key organizational habits that can remain constant during transitions, serving as stable points around which new routines can be built. These anchor habits help maintain a sense of control and continuity even when other aspects of life feel uncertain.

For example, when helping a young couple merge households, we identified their evening reset routine as their anchor habit. While many of their other organizational systems needed to be completely redesigned, maintaining this one consistent practice helped them stay grounded during the transition and provided a foundation for building new shared habits.

Transitions also present an excellent opportunity to reassess and potentially streamline your organizational systems. Often, what worked in one life phase might be unnecessarily complex for another. Use transitions as natural points for simplifying your habits and letting go of practices that no longer serve your current lifestyle.

Remember that the goal during transitions isn't to maintain perfect organization, but to preserve the core benefits of simplified living while adapting to new circumstances. By approaching transitions with flexibility and intention, you can maintain the essence of your organizational habits while allowing them to evolve with your changing life.

Measuring and Celebrating Progress

In the journey toward a simplified life, measuring and celebrating progress plays a vital role in maintaining motivation and reinforcing positive habits. Through my experience helping many friends maintain their downsizing success, I've discovered that acknowledging achievements, no matter how small, creates powerful momentum for continued growth.

One of my friends, David, initially struggled to recognize his progress because he focused solely on the end goal of a perfectly organized home. Together, we developed what we called the 'Victory Journal' – a simple but powerful tool for documenting both tangible and intangible wins in his downsizing journey. Each week, he would photograph one improved area and write a brief reflection about how the change impacted his daily life. Over time, this collection of before-and-after snapshots and personal insights became a powerful reminder of how far he'd come.

- Document visual progress through before-and-after photos

- Track time saved through improved organization

- Note positive changes in daily routines and stress levels

- Measure reduced cleaning and maintenance time

- Record compliments and observations from visitors

Measuring progress isn't just about counting items removed or spaces cleared – it's about recognizing the qualitative improvements in your life. While helping others with their downsizing journeys, I encourage them to notice subtle changes: the ease of finding important documents, reduced morning stress, or the simple pleasure of walking into an organized room.

Celebrating progress should be intentional rather than an afterthought. When working with families, I recommend creating celebration rituals that don't involve acquiring new things. For instance, one family I know would take a sunset walk together after completing each major decluttering milestone, using this time to reflect on their achievements and envision their next goals.

A particularly effective method I've seen work well is the 'Ripple Effect Review.' This involves noting not just direct organizational improvements, but also the secondary benefits that emerge. For example, someone might notice that maintaining an organized kitchen has led to more home-cooked meals, better food choices, and increased family dinner time.

- Schedule regular progress review sessions
- Create non-material rewards for reaching milestones
- Share successes with your support network
- Document unexpected benefits and positive changes
- Set and celebrate incremental goals

Remember that progress isn't always linear. There will be setbacks and challenges along the way, and acknowledging these as part of the journey is important. View occasional setbacks as valuable learning opportunities rather than failures.

One of the most powerful ways to measure progress is through what I call 'lifestyle indicators' – observable changes in daily habits and behaviors. These might include spending less time searching for items, making decisions more quickly about what to keep or discard, or feeling more comfortable inviting guests into your home spontaneously.

Celebrating progress also involves recognizing the emotional growth that comes with simplified living. Many people report feeling lighter, more confident, and more in control of their lives as they master the art of maintaining their simplified spaces. These intangible benefits often prove more meaningful than the physical transformations.

I've found that sharing progress with others can amplify the celebration and provide additional motivation. Whether through a simplicity circle, social media group, or family gathering, allowing others to witness and celebrate your achievements can strengthen your commitment to maintaining your simplified lifestyle.

Remember that each person's progress looks different, and comparisons to others rarely serve us well. Focus on your personal growth and the specific improvements that matter most in your life. By regularly acknowledging and celebrating your progress, you create positive reinforcement that supports your continued success in maintaining a simplified life.

As we conclude our exploration of sustaining a clutter-free transformation, remember that the journey toward simplified living is ongoing – a dynamic process that evolves with your life. Through the stories and strategies we've shared in this chapter, from Rachel's 'Sunset Reset' to Amanda's 'Sacred Space Protocol,' we've seen how small, consistent actions and thoughtful boundaries can create lasting change.

Maintaining a simplified life isn't about achieving perfection; it's about developing resilient habits and mindsets that flex with life's changes while preserving the serenity you've worked so hard to create. The daily maintenance rituals, clutter prevention mindset, and strong boundaries we've discussed form the foundation of sustainable organization, but it's the support systems and celebration of progress that truly transform these practices from obligations into lifestyle choices.

One of the most powerful lessons I've learned through helping friends and family maintain their downsizing success is that lasting transformation happens gradually, through the accumulation of small, mindful choices. Like tending a garden, maintaining a simplified life requires regular attention, but the rewards – reduced stress, increased mental clarity, and more time for what truly matters – make every effort worthwhile.

As you continue on your journey, remember that setbacks are a natural part of the process—and often valuable teachers. Life will bring its share of disruptions, and that's okay. The goal isn't perfect maintenance—it's a flexible, forgiving approach that allows you to gently return to your simplified practices whenever you need to. Your systems should feel like a support, not a constraint—something that enhances your life, not adds pressure to it.

The tools and strategies we've explored in this chapter—from simple daily rituals to thoughtful check-ins—offer more than just structure.

They provide a pathway to something deeper: freedom. Freedom from excess. Freedom from overwhelm. Freedom to live more fully in alignment with what truly matters to you.

As you move forward, trust the process. Celebrate your progress, no matter how small, and keep returning to the vision that inspired your downsizing journey in the first place. Each mindful habit, each intentional choice, contributes to something greater—a life that feels lighter, clearer, and more grounded in your values.

This isn't just about keeping things tidy. It's about creating a home—and a way of living—that supports who you are and who you're becoming. Your journey toward sustained simplicity is uniquely yours, and as you continue to refine your systems and adapt them to your life, you're building something meaningful and lasting: a foundation for a more intentional, more fulfilling way of living.

Conclusion

As we come to the close of this journey together, I'm reminded of my own path. What started as a simple goal to clear space became something much deeper: a journey of breaking generational patterns and creating the peaceful home I had always longed for. My story, like yours, reminds us that downsizing isn't just about reducing what we own—it's about opening the door to meaningful personal transformation.

Throughout this book, we've explored many layers of the downsizing experience—from understanding emotional attachments to building sustainable systems that support daily life. Along the way, we've discovered that successful downsizing isn't about rigid rules or forcing ourselves to live with less. It's about making thoughtful, values-based choices that support the life we truly want to create.

When the Fraser family realized that conventional organizing methods didn't suit their lively household, they found success by crafting a system that honored their unique rhythm. And Eleanor, who gently transformed her late husband's art studio from a space of sorrow into a legacy that would inspire future artists, reminds us that downsizing can be as much about healing as it is about organizing. These stories illustrate an essential truth: there is no one-size-fits-all approach to simplifying. The process is most powerful when it's deeply personal and grounded in what matters most to you.

The tools and strategies we've explored—from the 15-minute zones to the Sunset Reset routine—are more than just techniques. They're building blocks for a more intentional life. Like Miriam, who came to realize that her most treasured memories lived not in a box of old greeting cards, but in her heart, you too can find your own ways to honor your past while making space for your future.

As you continue along your downsizing journey, remember that this process isn't a race to the finish line—it's an ongoing evolution. There will be moments of doubt, emotional bumps in the road, and perhaps a few temporary setbacks. That's all part of it. But as the Thompson family discovered during their weekly "Sunday Circles," those challenges can become opportunities—moments for growth, reflection, and deeper connection.

The real measure of success isn't in how much you let go of—it's in how fully you're able to live with what remains. Whether you're just starting out or well along the path, every small step forward counts. Each thoughtful decision—whether it's choosing what to keep or gently releasing what no longer fits—is a powerful affirmation of the life you're creating.

So keep going, and do so with patience and self-compassion. Celebrate your progress. Learn from the hard moments. And always stay connected to your "why"—that inner reason that first sparked your desire for change. The insights you've gained through this process will extend far beyond your home. They'll shape how you make decisions, nurture relationships, and live with greater clarity and intention.

As you close this book and look ahead, remember: the joy of less isn't about what's missing—it's about what you've made room for. Your downsizing journey is ultimately about creating space—not just in your home, but in your heart and your life. Space to breathe. Space to grow. Space to dream and live more fully, in alignment with what truly matters to you.

May you move forward with confidence, knowing that you have the tools, the perspective, and the inner wisdom to continue building a simplified, intentional life. Because in the end, downsizing is not just a chapter—it's the beginning of something beautiful.

References

Becker, Joshua. (2016). The More of Less: Finding the Life You Want Under Everything You Own. WaterBrook.

Brownlee, Courtney. (2019). Digital Minimalism: Choosing a Focused Life in a Noisy World. Portfolio.

Fields, Scott. (2020). Downsizing the Family Home: What to Save, What to Let Go. Sterling.

Fortune, Regina. (2018). The Mindful Art of Swedish Death Cleaning: How to Free Yourself and Your Family from a Lifetime of Clutter. Scribner.

Jay, Francine. (2016). The Joy of Less: A Minimalist Guide to Declutter, Organize, and Simplify. Chronicle Books.

Kondo, Marie. (2014). The Life-Changing Magic of Tidying Up: The Japanese Art of Decluttering and Organizing. Ten Speed Press.

McGee, Peter. (2018). The Joy of Living with Less: How to Downsize to 100 Items and Why It's Worth It. Penguin Random House.

Moore, Gretchen. (2017). The Life-Changing Magic of Numbers: A Guide to Decluttering with the KonMari Method. Simon & Schuster.

Also by Sophie Alden

https://www.amazon.com/Calm-Within-Harnessing-Anxiety-Well-Being-ebook/dp/B0DXVW5358

Featuring Sophie Alden's Premiere DIY Book

Available through Amazon, Chapters Indigo, Barnes and Noble, Kobo, and Ingram Spark

About the author

SOPHIE ALDEN

Sophie Alden is a writer, researcher, and DIY enthusiast with a lifelong passion for health and wellness. An urban mom with a country soul, she escapes to nature whenever possible, embracing the best of both worlds. With a knack for turning curiosity into hands-on experience, Sophie shares practical wisdom and personal insights in her writing, always with a touch of warmth and humor.

Made in United States
North Haven, CT
26 June 2025